We few, we happy few, we band of brothers;
For he today that sheds his blood
With me shall be my brother.
Henry, VI, IV, iii

Only the dead
Have seen the end of war.
Plato

TO BE A U.S. MARINE

S.F. Tomajczyk

ZENITH
PRESS

To
Commander Charles F. Tomajczyk Jr., USN (Retired)
Captain E. Ross Mintz, MD, USND (Deceased)
Staff Sergeant David Pollard, USMC (Retired)
And to
All Marines
Who have given so much,
Expecting so little in return.
You keep us Free.
Semper Fidelis

First published in 2004 by Zenith Press, an imprint of MBI Publishing Company, 400 First Avenue North, Suite 300, Minneapolis, MN 55401 USA.

ISBN-13: 978-0-7603-1788-4

Edited by Steve Gansen
Designed by Russell S. Kuepper

Printed in China

On the cover: U.S. Marines from the 3rd Battalion, 4th Regiment, yell to urge infantrymen to rush across the damaged Baghdad Highway Bridge, Monday, April 7, 2003, as they move forward into the city while under fire in the southeastern outskirts of Baghdad. *Kuni Takahashi/Boston Herald/ReflexNews*

On the frontis: In the Marine Corps you expect to get down and dirty. As drill instructors constantly remind the filthy, tired recruits, "You don't have to like it, you just have to do it." With that mentality ingrained, it's no wonder these "grunts" get even the most difficult and ugly jobs done. *U.S. Marine Corps*

On the title page: A convoy of amphibious assault vehicles (AAVP7s) prepares to move inland after landing ashore. Already well ahead of them is the lead element of Marines, who arrived in earlier waves, and who were protected from the air by AH-1W Super Cobra attack helicopters and AV-8B Harrier "jump jets." Surprise, speed, and violence of attack are the tenets of modern warfare, and in this field, the Marine Corps is the best of the best. *S. F. Tomajczyk*

On the table of contents: Absolute perfection. This Marine drill instructor presently holds the highest scoring drill session in the Marine Corps – a feat easier said than done. It requires total focus and sharp, precise moves with sword that literally "hiss" through the air when carried out. *U.S. Marine Corps*

On the back cover: The so-called "fog of battle" is real—but in this case it is intentionally caused by a heavy obscuring smoke. Marine recruits learn to conduct missions in such an environment so one day when they find themselves on the battlefield they will know how to deal with the confusion and low visibility, as well as the choking and lacrimation caused by the smoke itself. *U.S. Marine Corps.* **Back Cover 2:** The Marine Corps' missions are so spread out and global in nature that when Marines watch the sun set over the horizon in one country, other Marines actually watch it rise over the horizon in another nation. Their presence around the world helps preserve America's democratic way of life while simultaneously bringing peace and the hope of freedom to others. *U.S. Marine Corps.*
Back Cover 3: It was through the dedication and blood of Marines that helped the United States of America become a nation. The Marine Corps was actually established by the founding fathers to help the struggling colonists gain their freedom from England. *U.S. Marine Corps*

About the author

A graduate of the University of Michigan and the New York Institute of Photography, S. F. Tomajczyk is an author and photographer who specializes in military affairs, counterterrorism, and homeland security issues. Including this book, he is the author of 11 nonfiction titles, including *Carrier Battle Group*, *Black Hawk*, and *US Elite Counterterrorist Forces*. His work has appeared in a variety of publications and television shows, including *People* magazine, *NBC Dateline*, and *Extra*.

Over the years Tomajczyk has flown with the International Ice Patrol searching for rogue icebergs, tailhooked aboard the USS *John F. Kennedy* (CV-67), and shot off the bow of the USS *George Washington* (CVN-73). He has also participated in a mock amphibious assault against the fictional nation of Korona, photographed Navy SEALs in training, qualified as a sharpshooter with the MP-5 submachine gun, worn bomb suits, and learned how improvised explosive devices are rendered safe. Further, he has flown nap-of-the-earth aboard the FBI Hostage Rescue Team's "little bird" helicopter.

Tomajczyk is listed in *Who's Who in America* and *Contemporary Authors*, and is professionally affiliated with the Author's Guild, American Society of Media Photographers, International Association of Emergency Managers, and the International Association of Counterterrorism and Security Professionals. He resides in the "Live Free or Die" state of New Hampshire.

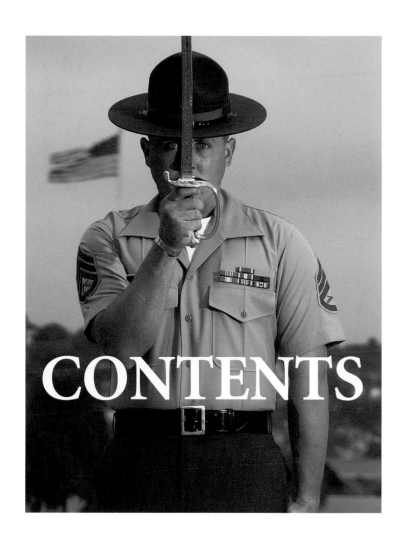

CONTENTS

Preface

THE FEW. THE PROUD.

*The Marine Corps has just been called by the
New York Times, "The elite of this country."
I think it is the elite of the world.*

Admiral William Halsey, U.S. Navy

T"This has to be the most intimidating and anal place on earth," I muttered aloud, the hair on my neck standing on end. It was mid-November and I was driving across the narrow two-lane land bridge that connects the mainland of South Carolina with the offshore, mosquito-infested swamp known as Parris Island. A large sign ominously read: "We Make Marines." Every 150 feet along the causeway a pair of immaculately groomed palm trees stood at rigid attention—one on either side of the road, neither daring to move even an inch in the wind. I counted 30 pairs of these silent sentries guarding the path to the heart of the United States Marine Corps.

The effect was so menacing and somber I felt as if I were in J. R. R. Tolkien's *The Lord of the Rings*, entering the Land of Mordor where the sleepless eye of Sauron searches far and wide, missing nothing. I fully expected winged Black Riders to swoop down behind me at any second.

I was taken aback by my reaction. After all, my father had been a career naval officer, which meant I had spent much of my youth living on or visiting military bases. Furthermore, most Navy bases have a contingent of Marines stationed within the barbed wire, so it was not as if I had never seen a "Leatherneck" before. As a matter of fact, I had often played with friends, jumping, crawling, and climbing on the Marines' obstacle course, as well as occupying empty camouflaged trenches in the woods where the Marines held combat maneuvers.

Yet, in spite of my familiarity with the military life, Parris Island was alien to me. None of the bases I knew

The so-called "fog of battle" is real—but in this case it is intentionally caused by a heavy obscuring smoke. Marine recruits learn to conduct missions in such an environment so when they one day find themselves on the battlefield they will know how to deal with the confusion and low visibiltiy, as well as the choking and lacrimation caused by the smoke itself. *U.S. Marine Corps*

It was through the dedication and blood of Marines that helped the United States of America become a nation. The Marine Corps was actually established by the founding fathers to help the struggling colonists gain their freedom from England. *U.S. Marine Corps*

compared with it. Not only is "PI" immaculate (everything has its proper, assigned place), but the very atmosphere reeks with a stern, unyielding, no-nonsense aura.

Within seconds of driving down the causeway, I suddenly understood the unspoken metaphor: The path to becoming a United States Marine is long *and* narrow. There is absolutely no margin for error. Travel a bit too far to the left or right, and you end up in the alligator-infested waters. So commit; focus; succeed.

And thus I began to sense the difference between the Marine Corps and the other armed services—failure is simply not an option. The word "try" is not in their vocabulary. A Marine *does*. And he or she does it coolly and capably.

This creed haunted me throughout my visit at PI and far beyond as I researched, photographed, and wrote this book. In the back of my mind I heard the whisper of 229 years of Marines in the Corps reminding me, "Do it right. Valor. Honor. Loyalty."

As a result, *To Be a U.S. Marine* is admittedly the most difficult book I have written to date. It is not a book about Marine history. It is not a book about Marine weapons and equipment. And it is not a book about Marine traditions. Rather, it is a book that blends all three together, thereby presenting a broad cross-section of the modern Marine Corps in the hope of unveiling the reasons it is so unique among the military branches. *To Be a U.S. Marine* also dedicates about a third of its pages to the rite of passage young men and women endure to earn—yes, *earn*—the "Globe and Anchor" and, along with it, the title of Marine. For it is that arduous and painful journey that enables us all to gain a better appreciation as to what makes a Marine a Marine.

Loudon, N.H.
June 2004

Acknowledgments

Without question, this book would not have been possible without the assistance of the following individuals and organizations, who contributed not only their own expertise, but also vital information at a time when our country was fighting a global war on terrorism while simultaneously attempting to inject democracy into war-torn Iraq: General Michael W. Hagee, USMC, Commandant of the Marine Corps; Brigadier General Mary Ann Krusa-Dossin, USMC, director of public affairs, Headquarters, U.S. Marine Corps; Lieutenant Colonel S. H. Kay, USMC, deputy director of public affairs, Headquarters, U.S. Marine Corps; Major Douglas M. Powell, USMC, media branch director, Headquarters U.S. Marine Corps.

The following personnel at MCRD Parris Island were of assistance: Lieutenant Colonel Kim C. Johnson, USMC, commanding officer, 4th Recruit Training Battalion, MCRD, Parris Island; Major Kenneth D. White, USMC, public affairs director; Captain James R. Nott, USMC, deputy public affairs officer; Master Sergeant Arturo Prioletta, USMC, Public Affairs Office; Captain J. D. Arico, USMC, assistant operations officer, Recruit Training Regiment; Chief Warrant Officer Martin Dankanich, USMC, range officer/OIC A-Line, Range Co WFTBN; Major Diana L. Staneszewski, USMC, operations officer, Recruit Training Regiment; Sharon Henderson, community relations specialist, Public Affairs Office; Corporal Virgil P. Richardson, media chief; Stephen R. Wise, Ph.D., museum curator, Parris Island Museum.

Also of assistance were: Lieutenant Colonel Rick Long, USMC, director of public affairs, Quantico Marine Corps Base; Captain Jeff Landis, USMC, public affairs officer, Quantico Marine Corps Base; Captain Teresa Ovalle, USMC, public affairs media section, Camp Lejeune; Sergeant Mandy McCammon, USMC, public affairs media section, Camp Lejeune; Staff Sergeant Wesley Guarino, USMC, Marine Corps Recruiting Office,

Concord, New Hampshire; Captain Burell, USMC, executive officer, Marine Corps Recruiting Office, Manchester, New Hampshire; Gunnery Sergeant Timothy McGough, USMC, public affairs, New York; Captain Jaret Heil, USMC, XO, public affairs, New York; Major David Anderson, USMC, director, public affairs, New York; Captain Jerome Bryant, USMC, media officer, Quantico Marine Corps Air Base.

I also wish to acknowledge Brigadier General Walter E. Gaskin, USMC, former commanding officer of the 22nd MEU (SOC); Rear Admiral Stephen C. Jasper, USN, former commodore of Amphibious Squadron Six; Naval Sea Systems Command; U.S. Marine Corps History and Museums Division; U.S. Marine Corps Mountain Warfare Training Center; U.S. Marine Corps Amphibious Reconnaissance School; U.S. Marine Corps Combat Development Command; U.S. Marine Corps Warfighting Laboratory; U.S. Marine Corps Training and Education Command; U.S. Marine Corps Futures Warfare Division; U.S. Marine Corps Doctrine Division; U.S. Marine Corps Expeditionary Warfare School; U.S. Marine Corps Scout-Sniper School; U.S. Marine Corps the Basic School; U.S. Marine Corps Helicopter Squadron One (HMX-1); U.S. Navy Office of Information; U.S. Navy Joint Strike Fighter Program; Kodak Professional Services; Fuji Film; Michael Moore and John R. Kent, F-35 JSF Communications Office, Lockheed-Martin Aeronautics Co.; Northrop Grumman Corporation; Raytheon Company; Mike Maus, public affairs specialist, COMNAVAIRLANT; Barry Higginbotham, deputy for media, CINCLANTFLT; JOC David Rourk, media action officer, CINCLANTFLT; OSCM(SW) Delta Hinson, NAVPHIBASE Little Creek; and the crews of the USS *Nassau* (LHA-4); USS *George Washington* (CVN-73); USS *John F. Kennedy* (CV-67); USS *Bataan* (LHD-5) and LCAC-84 of Assault Craft Unit 4.

And last, I want to thank my grandfather, Captain E. Ross Mintz, M.D., USNR (deceased), who captured my imagination as a child with stories about his exploits as a field surgeon in the Central Pacific during World War II, serving with the Marines' III Amphibious Corps as they conducted the landings on Peleliu, Guam, and Okinawa. His USMC-issued jungle machete and rifle bayonet are both proudly displayed in my office, along with his Bronze Star.

He was the best of the "Devil Docs" and was up for promotion to rear admiral when an auto accident left him paralyzed. In spite of the handicap—and in true tradition of the Corps he so admired—he never allowed his paralysis to interfere with his life. He continued to drive, and he traveled the world to be with my family as we transferred from one military base to another. It was he who taught me to "reach for the stars, because if you only reach for the roof you never get off the ground." It is an adage I've followed ever since . . . and I have the stardust to prove it. Thanks, "Skipper."

ONE

Marines laden with combat gear march aboard a CH-53E Super Stallion heavy-lift assault helicopter. It can transport up to 55 Marines (or 24 litters and four attendants) or a 36,000-pound underslung load of heavy equipment, such as a howitzer. *Department of Defense*

First to Fight

Saepius Externus. Semper Fidelis. Frater Infinitas.
Often Tested. Always Faithful. Brothers Forever.

I can see the possibility we might be able to live without the Army, without a Navy—we might be able to live without the Air Force—but this country can never live without a corps of lean, mean Marines.
Honorable David Packard

The United States Marine Corps is actually older than the nation it ferociously defends. Neither soldier nor sailor, Marines (and that's with a capital "M" they remind you) are sea-based, combat-ready warriors who attack the enemy by land, by air, and from the sea—simultaneously. As a result, the Marine Corps is America's only elite fighting force in and of itself.

Certainly the Navy has its SEALs, and the Army has its Green Berets, but both are highly trained specialty units within their own branches. In the Marine Corps on the other hand, all 177,000 are trained as elite fighters who routinely go where others fear to tread. Over the past two centuries, Marines have participated in every major and minor engagement that the United States has been involved in, fighting battles aboard ships, on distant shores, and in steamy jungles and hot deserts to defend our nation's interests and to preserve our democratic way of life.

Although it is the smallest of all America's armed forces, the Marine Corps does, in fact, have a global presence and a global reach. Marines are so spread out around the world today that some can watch the sun set while others are watching it rise.

But it nearly did not happen . . .

RICKETY BEGINNINGS

On November 10, 1775, the Second Continental Congress, which was meeting in Philadelphia to create what would soon become the United States of America, passed a resolution sponsored by John Adams stating that two battalions of Marines "be inlisted and commissioned to serve for and during the present war between Great Britain and the colonies." At the time, things were not going well for the rebelling colonists, who had earlier declared their independence from England. The battle-hardened and well-organized British forces were effectively strangling the resistance. In fact, at the time, George Washington's Continental Army had yet to win a victory on the battlefield. It was having a difficult time finding volunteer soldiers and obtaining adequate supplies of food, clothing, ammunition, and weapons.

By raising two battalions of Continental Marines, the fledgling nation hoped to use them as landing forces with the naval fleet and turn the tide against the British. At sea, the Marines scrambled like spiders up the rigging to the "fighting tops" of the masted warships, where they blasted the decks of enemy ships with grenades and musket fire.

The commanding officer of these battalions was 30-year-old Captain Samuel Nicholas, a patriot and a Quaker, who became the Marine Corps' first commissioned officer and, over time, eventually was recognized as the Marine Corps' first commandant. In early 1776, Captain Nicholas and 234 newly recruited Continental Marines set sail aboard eight warships under the command of Commodore Esek Hopkins to clear the waters off America's mid-Atlantic coast of all British warships. As part of this plan—and to acquire needed weapons and gunpowder for the war effort—the fleet conducted a daring raid against the rich British crown colony of New Providence in the Bahamas.

On the afternoon of March 3, 1776, Captain Nicholas and a landing party of Marines rowed ashore on whaleboats and moved inland to challenge Fort Montagu and Fort Nassau, both of which were defended by small contingents of British soldiers. The subsequent fighting was very light, and in the end the Continental Marines handily captured 46 cannons and 24 barrels of gunpowder. Thereafter known as the "Gunpowder Expedition," the event denoted the U.S. Marine Corps' first amphibious landing—a technique that remains a trademark of the service to this day.

Although the Continental Marines distinguished themselves in a number of important military operations on land and at sea during the American Revolution, the Treaty of Paris (1783) effectively threatened their existence with the ending of hostilities and the recognition of the United States as a nation. With no war to be fought, there was no longer any need to maintain a large and expensive military force. Besides, America's founding fathers were reluctant to have a standing army that could potentially be used in the future by a president for despotic purposes. And so Congress voted to disband much of the nation's armed forces.

And it was here that the Marine Corps learned a lesson that continues to occasionally haunt Marines today: They were respected, but not necessarily wanted.

As legend tells it, after months of negotiation between the Army and the Navy over how the remaining resources should be divided as a result of the downsizing, all that was left were some mules and the two battalions of Continental Marines. With a flip of a coin to settle the debate, the Army commander won. He took the mules.

The jettisoned Marines remained with the Navy but, since it had sold its frigates and ships-of-the-line, there essentially was no need for them and the process of discharging them from service began in earnest. The last Marine officer was discharged in September 1783, leaving the youthful eight-year-old Corps in existence by name only.

This could have heralded the end of the so-called "sea soldiers," the sun setting on their North American horizon. Fortunately, peace is a rare condition, having existed only about five percent of the time throughout history. (In fact, at any given time today, there are 40 to 100 armed conflicts being fought somewhere on the planet.) On July 11, 1798, Congress resuscitated the Marine Corps under the command of Major William Ward Burrows, a Philadelphian who had fought in the American Revolution. He quickly commissioned 25 officers and recruited 58 enlisted men to participate in the naval war being waged with France at the time.

Given the opportunity to have a second life, the Marine Corps took up the advance and never looked back. Adopting the dictum *Anytime. Anywhere.*, the Corps quickly established itself as a small, highly skilled body of warriors who were prepared at any time—and on short notice—to storm the beaches. They focused on warfare, a forward-deployed presence, and a rapid crisis-response

Marines of the 26th MEU/SOC, who are operating out of a forward base near Kandahar, Afghanistan, head out across the desolate terrain to the front lines to secure the perimeter in support of Operation Enduring Freedom. As is usual, they serve as human mules, grunting under the load of their packs, which weigh more than 50 pounds. *U.S. Navy*

capability—all of which made the Marine Corps the natural military force for the president of the United States to turn to when a crisis arose.

Ironically, most of the world's crises over the past two centuries have been spawned where the land meets the sea—a region referred to as the littorals. It is the same environment the Marines have come to specialize in. More than half the world's population and three-quarters of its cities are located in these regions, creating enormous zones of commerce. As a result, the littorals are vital to the world's economies.

By specializing in amphibious warfare, the Marine Corps is America's only branch of service that is trained and equipped to conduct expeditionary operations by air, land, or sea—a niche the Army, Navy, and Air Force are not able to fill. This positioning has proven especially invaluable in the post-World War II era when Congress has considered—on several occasions—downsizing the military, just as it did after the American Revolution, to reduce federal budgetary pressures.

In one memorable speech before the Senate Committee on Naval Affairs in 1946, General Alexander A. Vandegrift, 18th commandant of the Marine Corps, methodically and passionately defended the Marine Corps' right to exist. Among his many points, he said the Corps was an organic element of the nation's fighting fleet, prepared to immediately deploy on the battlefield. As such it represented a "powerful source of ready strength to the nation, both in war and in peace." Unlike the Army, ponderous and deliberately organized for staying power in a theater of war, the Marine Corps was the proverbial tip of the spear—a swift and mobile force

Marines take up defensive positions at the Kandahar airport after shots have been fired. The gunfire erupted just after a C-17 transport took off with 20 Al Qaeda and Taliban detainees on board. The glow in the photo is light coming from an illumination grenade.

A ground combat element of Marines from the 31st MEU/SOC, which is based in Okinawa, Japan, lands in a field in Thailand as part of a live-fire training exercise. The tandem-rotor CH-46 Sea Knight helicopter has been the primary combat assault helicopter of the Marine Corps since 1964. It will be replaced by the tilt-rotor MV-22 Osprey.

ready to be the first to fight. Vandegrift gave several examples where the Army arrived on the scene only *after* the objective had already been accomplished by Marines, including Guadalcanal in 1942. He mocked, ". . . no matter how hard it tries, a great national army can not be a specialist Marine Corps and still be an army."

And last, the general pointed out that contrary to what the Senate committee had heard from the War Department (predecessor of today's Department of Defense), there was no duplication between the Army and the Marine Corps. The Army, he noted, had never been in the amphibious field, and did not have the schools or the training facilities to do so. In fact, Army troops that had taken part in landing operations during World War II had simply applied the techniques and equipment developed by the Marine Corps and Navy. In many instances, they had actually been trained by the Marine Corps.

In the end, General Vandegrift—in true spirit of the Marine Corps—refused to beg for the Corps' existence, allowing its heritage and laurels to speak for themselves. "We have pride in ourselves and in our past," Vandegrift

concluded, "but we do not rest our case on any presumed ground of gratitude owing us from the nation. The bended knee is not a tradition of our Corps."

The committee agreed, and the Marine Corps remains to this day America's "Force in Readiness."

FIGHTING IN EVERY CLIME AND PLACE

Due to the diversity of environs the Marine Corps must operate in—land, air, and sea—and successfully employ warfighting tactics appropriate to each unique situation, its role in the defense of the United States is both important and complex. Among the Corps' many mandates and missions are to:

Right: Marines sit alert atop an LAV-25 armored vehicle, heading off on patrol near Kandahar, Afghanistan. An AH-1W Super Cobra attack helicopter zooms overhead, providing close-air support. It has a 295-mile range when carrying its basic combat attack load. *U.S. Navy*

Below: Fire belches from the muzzle of an M198 155mm medium howitzer as an artillery round pays a visit to Saddam Hussein's army in north Umm Qasr, Iraq, during Operation Iraqi Freedom in March 2003. The weapon can fire a maximum of four rounds per minute, or two rounds per minute in sustained firing.

- Develop doctrines, tactics, techniques, and equipment to be used by landing forces in amphibious operations
- Provide Marines and equipment for airborne operations, as needed
- Seize or defend forward naval bases
- Provide Marines for service on armed vessels of the U.S. Navy
- Provide Marines for security of property at naval stations and bases, including nuclear weapons
- Provide Marine forces to protect U.S. embassies and consulates overseas
- Assign Marine forces to Unified and Specified commands, as directed
- Be prepared to expand peacetime components of the Marine Corps to meet the needs of war
- Perform other duties as the President of the United States directs

The last directive is particularly noteworthy, because it means the Marine Corps—unlike its sister services—takes orders directly from the President and is answerable to him. It also signifies that Marines can be used for non–naval events, such as humanitarian aid missions, *in extremis* hostage rescue, civilian evacuation, and counterterrorism operations. As a result, we have witnessed the Marines in recent years restoring order in Haiti after the resignation of president Jean-Bertrand Aristide, evacuating embassy personnel from Liberia during a local rebellion, providing aid to earthquake victims in Turkey, and attacking Al Qaeda and Taliban elements in Afghanistan during Operation Enduring Freedom.

From an organizational standpoint, the Marine Corps is one of two military services in America's naval establishment—the U.S. Navy and the U.S. Marine Corps—both of which are under the command of the secretary of the Navy. The National Security Act (1947, as

An all-terrain LAV-AT armored vehicle configured in the antitank role speeds down a dirt road at dawn. It serves as an agile platform that supports infantry and reconnaissance forces by taking out enemy armored vehicles, including tanks. Immediately behind the LAV commander in this photo is a TOW II launcher, which holds and fires two wire-guided antitank missiles. The vehicle carries a total of 16 missiles.

Marines conduct nuclear, biological, and chemical training with the Javelin missile system at Camp Coyote, Kuwait, during Operation Enduring Freedom. The Javelin is a lightweight, fire-and-forget antitank weapon that has a range of 6,000 feet. It uses an imaging-infrared seeker to attack a tank or armored combat vehicle from the top.

amended) requires that the combatant forces of the Marine Corps be organized on the basis of three Marine divisions and three air wings, and limits its peacetime size to no more than 400,000. (The only time the Corps ever came close to this number was during the Vietnam War in 1969, when there were 309,771 Marines in the Corps. Today, that figure hovers in the 175,000 range.) The Commandant of the Marine Corps commands the Corps as a whole and is responsible to the secretary of the Navy for its readiness and total performance.

Considering the Marine Corps has walked the decks of warships since its inception in 1775, it is not surprising that its relationship with the Navy is tightly knit and enduring. The Navy is responsible for transporting the Marines to the battlefield and providing protective naval gunfire support so the Marine combat units can quickly move inland to their objective. The Navy also offers medical care through its corpsmen, who are specially trained by the Marines to accompany them in a war zone. In return, the Marine Corps assists the Navy with such things as intelligence collection, combat cargo operations, military operations, and security, both ashore and afloat.

Examples of the security function include contingents of Marines guarding so-called "King Tut" nuclear weapons bunkers at naval weapons stations, restricting access to nuclear submarine bases, and watching over suspected terrorists detained at Camp Delta at Guantanamo Bay, Cuba. Marines also protect vital areas of an aircraft carrier, such as the Flag Battle Center, where combat decisions are made by the carrier battle group's commander (usually an admiral) and his staff.

The beauty—and lethality!—of the Marine Corps lies with its size and organization. Adhering to the concept of expeditionary maneuver warfare, the Corps proactively positions its forces around the world in locations where they can quickly respond when needed. One way of achieving this is to send an Amphibious Ready Group—which comprises several amphibious ships and more than 2,000 Marines—to a region before tensions between chest-pounding nations explode. The Marines are self-contained; they bring everything they need to wage war with them, including the infamous "three Bs": beans, bullets, and bandages. Their unique command, control, communications, intelligence, and logistics capabilities also allow them to operate independently when necessary. The Marines rely on no one but themselves. As a result, Marine forces maneuver quickly and decisively with the deadly intent of surprising the enemy and shattering its cohesion. It is the

Above: Marines peek over the lip of their assault amphibian vehicle (AAVP7) to watch the destruction of enemy 120mm mortar rounds that were captured in an Iraqi truck in Al Fajr, Iraq. The AAVP7 can transport up to 21 combat-equipped Marines who, as this photo shows, drape their belongings all over it. Doing so provides extra protection from shrapnel and bullets.

Left: A scout-sniper team trudges through sliding dirt to move into a shooting position to provide protection to a Marine element as it takes a brief halt on its way to Baghdad. Both Marines are wearing armored vests, as well as knee-pads that are pushed down to their ankles—available for quick use.

Right: An M1A1 Abrams tank conducts live-fire training somewhere in the Persian Gulf region in late 2003. The tank is assigned to the 13th MEU/SOC which, in turn, is part of the newly created Expeditionary Strike Group One (ESG-1). An ESG is a naval strike force designed to equip amphibious forces with added firepower.

proverbial "hit and run" tactic. Often the enemy is so quickly overwhelmed that he never knows exactly what happened. We have witnessed this time and again.

For instance, on the first day of the ground war to liberate Kuwait in 1991, the 1st Marine Division, positioned near the Persian Gulf, surged across a heavily fortified berm that most experts considered impenetrable. Using artillery, tanks, and bulldozers, the Marines blasted and plowed right through the berm—wiping out the minefields and tank traps—and continued advancing against the Iraqi army. By evening, the Marines had met every objective expected of them and had captured more than 16,000 Iraqis in the process. Less than 90 hours later, the 1st Marine Division was in Kuwait City.

A similar scenario played itself out in the 2003 Gulf War (Operation Iraqi Freedom) to liberate the people of Iraq from Saddam Hussein's dictatorial regime. In the opening days of the war and operating on little or no sleep, the Marines maneuvered and fought inland so rapidly that they nearly outran their own combat logistical support teams, which provided food, gasoline, and ammunition. Again, the Iraqi soldiers never knew what hit them. As one Marine is alleged to have muttered with disdain, "I hope they're better lovers, 'cause they sure can't fight."

The U.S. Marine Corps may indeed be America's smallest military force, but its fierce, no-nonsense approach to combat has earned the Corps the reputation of being a

A High-Mobility, Multipurpose Wheeled Vehicle (HMMWV)—or "Humvee" to civilians—races to support fellow Marines in a fire-fight in Nasiriyah, Iraq, during Operation Iraqi Freedom. The vehicle has a .50-caliber machine gun attached to it.

A Marine squad leader with the 15th MEU/SOC moves his Marines to their objective during a mission in support of Operation Iraqi Freedom. In the void of the desert, the Marines take up positions where they can—even if it is behind a sand dune.

MOTTOS OF THE MARINE CORPS

Fortitudine (With Fortitude) — Adopted after the War of 1812
Per Mare, Per Terram (By Sea and By Land)
From the Halls of Montezuma to the Shores of Tripoli — Adopted 1848
Semper Fidelis (Always Faithful) — Adopted 1883

Source: U.S. Marine Corps History and Museums Division

A sniper from a surveillance and target acquisition platoon uses the scope on his M40A3 rifle to check out a suspicious-acting Iraqi, to make certain he is not carrying a missile launcher or rocket-propelled grenade launcher.

Using the night vision goggles (NVG) attached to his helmet, a Marine stands guard while his fellow Marines search a house for weapon stockpiles in Karbala, Iraq, in July 2003. The NVGs amplify existing light, turning the world into shades of green.

CUSTOMS AND TRADITIONS OF THE MARINE CORPS

- In Washington, D.C., the license plate of the Commandant of the Marine Corps is "1775."
- Since the 1920s, an English bulldog has been the official mascot of the Marine Barracks in Washington, D.C.
- If a Marine officer enters a mess without removing his hat, he or she is liable to buy a round of drinks for everyone present. The exception to this rule is if the officer is on duty and under arms.
- All Marine posts (and even some camps in the field) have a bell, usually from a decommissioned U.S. Navy warship.
- The Marine Corps celebrates its birthday every November 10, and it is the top social occasion of the year. A cake, if included as part of the ceremony, is cut with a Mameluke sword, and slices are presented by the senior Marine to the youngest and oldest Marines present.
- The top of a Marine officer's hat is decorated with an embroidered *quatrefoil*, a cross-shaped braid. This design was allegedly added in 1859 so that Marine snipers in the rigging of a ship could more easily identify their own officers on the deck below—and not shoot them.
- When Marines enter a boat or vehicle, the junior person goes first and takes the less desirable places in the middle or front. When debarking, the senior leaves first, while juniors follow in order of rank.
- The slogan *First to Fight* has been on recruiting posters since World War I.
- The "Marine Corps Hymn" is the oldest of the official songs of the Armed Services.
- The so-called "Mameluke sword," which has been used by Marine officers since 1826, is the weapon with the longest service in the U.S. military. The sword gets its name from the cross-hilt and ivory grip, both of which originated in Arabia and North Africa. The second longest service goes to the ceremonial swords carried by Marine sergeants, a tradition that began in 1850.
- The red-colored leg stripe on a Marine's Dress Blue uniform is known as the "Blood Stripe," in remembrance of the Marines who stormed Chapultepec Castle in Mexico City during a bloody battle in 1847.
- Every New Year's Day since 1869, the Marine Band has serenaded the Commandant of the Marine Corps at his quarters. Afterward, the band members are invited inside for breakfast and hot-buttered rum.
- Mess Night is a formal dinner with all members or the officers of a particular post or unit. It is often held on special anniversaries or to honor a distinguished guest. At some Mess Nights the Marines emulate the Continental Marines by drinking toasts of "1775 Rum Punch," which is made up of four parts dark rum, two parts lime juice, one part pure maple syrup, and a small amount of grenadine syrup to taste.
- If a Marine unsheathes a sword inside a mess or wardroom, he or she must buy a round of drinks for all present. This tradition helped prevent dueling in the early days of the Navy and Marine Corps.
- According to Navy Regulations (1865), Marines—other than the ship's captain—are always the last to leave a ship being abandoned or decommissioned.
- The phrase "Tell it to the Marines" allegedly comes from King Charles II, who was shocked to learn about flying fish from a sea captain. He turned to a member of the Maritime Regiment (precursor of the Royal Marines) and asked if it was true. The colonel confirmed it, whereupon Charles II decreed that from then on anytime a strange thing was presented, ". . . we will tell it to the Marines, for they go everywhere and see everything, and if they say it is so, we will believe it."
- All Marines salute a Medal of Honor recipient, regardless of rank.
- A Marine will fight and die rather than permit the national colors (i.e., U.S. flag) or a Marine Corps color to be dishonored or captured. If capture seems likely, the flags are burned.

lean and mean, fast-moving fighting machine. And since it uses an elastic organizational structure (as will be discussed in Chapter Three), the Marines can quickly expand and tailor their forces in the field to address a particular threat and then, just as quickly, contract. They are indeed the "Incredible Hulks" of warfare.

THE MARINE MYSTIQUE

Over the centuries since its birth, the reach of the Marine Corps has extended from the shores of North America over the horizon to the entire world. And just as quickly, Marines have earned universal respect and prestige. When the Marines land, the local populace often line the streets to welcome them, while combatants scramble to give them wide berth.

A story is told that during the crisis in Mogadishu, Somalia, in 1991, a group of armed Somalis marched up to the U.S. Embassy, demanding that the gates be thrown open or they would attack. When they looked up at the embassy walls, they saw Marines aiming their weapons down at them. "Excuse me," said the leader of the group, holding up his hands. "I didn't mean it. My mistake. I thought you were Army."

That instantaneous respect is not uncommon. During Operation Iraqi Freedom, for instance, Iraqi soldiers quickly learned that Marines rolled their shirt sleeves up on the outside; Army soldiers, on the inside. They used that fashion quirk to avoid shooting at Marines, knowing that if they did pull the trigger, the Marines would immediately retaliate with massive firepower. (Marines, unlike Army

A stash of 155mm artillery rounds stands prepared to be fired at Iraqi targets during Operation Iraqi Freedom. The M198 howitzer can fire conventional rounds like these up to about 14 miles, and rocket-assisted projectiles up to 18.6 miles.

The Marine Corps often serves as a flag honor guard during public events, such as this National Football League game.

The Marine Band from Quantico, Virginia, performs at Carnegie Hall in New York City. The band was part of the September 11 Memorial Concert to raise funds for the New York Police Department and Marine Corps Scholarship charities.

Sergeant Major Alfred McMichael (right) stands before General Michael W. Hagee, Commandant of the Marine Corps (left), after relinquishing his title of sergeant major of the Marine Corps—the highest enlisted position in the Corps. The ceremony took place at Marine Barracks, Eighth and I, in Washington, D.C.

HISTORICAL EMBLEMS OF THE MARINE CORPS

1776—A silver (or pewter) anchor fouled with rope.
1834—A brass eagle.
1859—A wreath that partially encompassed the bottom section of the Great Shield of the United States. On the shield was a hunting horn (traditional symbol of light infantry) with the letter "M" inscribed inside the bugle.
1868—A gold "foul anchor" resting on its side and surmounted by a globe of the world showing the western hemisphere. A spread eagle sits atop the globe with a scroll inscribed "Semper Fidelis" in its beak. This "Globe and Anchor" emblem was adopted by Brigadier General Jacob Zeilin, the seventh Commandant of the Marine Corps.

The U.S. Marine Corps emblem is arguably the most important insignia a Marine wears. It is worn by private and general alike, and it clearly shows that the Corps is both American and maritime. The emblem is the unique symbol that immediately identifies its wearer as having *earned* the title of U.S. Marine and as being a member of the "Few and the Proud" brotherhood.

With regard to the 1868 emblem, which is still used to this day, many Marines say they arrived at the design in the following manner: "We stole the eagle from the Air Force, the anchor from the Navy, the rope (which fouls the anchor) from the Army, and on the seventh day when God rested, we overran His perimeter and stole the globe, and have been protecting our shores ever since."

The attacks of September 11, 2001, triggered a global war against terrorism. This photo was taken by Gunnery Sergeant Matthew T. Olivolo, USMC, who was serving at Recruiting Station New York when the attack occurred. Within minutes of the second tower being struck, he pulled his car over at Staten Island Harbor to photograph the scene. Upon arriving at the recruiting station—which was located just four blocks from the World Trade Center—he and other Marines helped first responders set up a medical-triage facility.

soldiers, do not have to get permission to return fire and attack. They are empowered by their superiors to handle a situation any way they see fit.)

As an aside, one humorous incident occurred during the 1993 Los Angeles riots. A police officer reportedly asked a group of Marines who were helping restore order to the city to "cover" him as he ran across the street. Without question and with a nod of their heads they did so, letting loose with a hailstorm of machine-gun bullets, just as they had been trained at the School of Infantry.

So what is it that gives the Marine Corps its special aura? What makes it so very distinct from any other military service, almost a breed unto itself? After all, one sees more USMC bumper stickers on vehicles, and more USMC flags flying in front of homes than any other service.

The answer is complex. While the Corps is a military force, it is much more. You can be in the Navy. You can be in the Air Force. And you can be in the Army. But, you *are* a Marine. And whereas the Air Force chief of staff would never be called *airman* and the chief of naval operations would never be called *sailor*, the Commandant of the Marine Corps *would* be proud to be called *Marine*. In fact, everyone in the Marine Corps, from the lowest private to the most senior general, is a Marine, and damn proud of it.

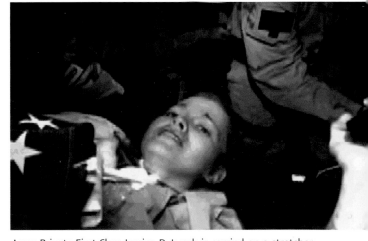

Army Private First Class Jessica D. Lynch is carried on a stretcher to an awaiting helicopter after being rescued from her Iraqi captors. She was captured after her maintenance convoy was ambushed in the southern Iraqi city of Nasiriyah in March 2003. A joint team consisting of Army Rangers, Air Force combat controllers, Navy SEALs, and Marines participated in the rescue effort. Two Marines piloted a CH-46E Sea Knight from the USS *Boxer* as part of the mission. Additionally, a Force Reconnaissance Marine received the Bronze Star for valor for leading his unit while gathering intelligence for the mission, setting up the helicopter landing zone, and placing snipers in position to protect the raid force. *Department of Defense*

A Marine corporal (right) points out the lateral firing limits for the Mk. 19 40mm grenade launcher, which is being used here to protect a Marine defensive position at Camp Ripper, Kuwait, during Operation Iraqi Freedom. The Mk. 19 can fire a wide variety of grenades, including armor-piercing, fragmentation, and illumination rounds. It has a range of more than 6,000 feet and can fire 40 rounds per minute, sustained.

They are convinced that serving as a Marine is the highest privilege, firmly believing that the Corps is second to none and that it is arguably the most elite military body on the face of the planet. Every Marine wraps himself or herself in the Corps' long tradition of service and sacrifice, and adheres to an uncompromising code of honor, courage, commitment, discipline, and personal integrity.

Ask any Marine what he or she loves about the Corps, and you are likely to hear answers like:
- The toughest drill instructors in the world
- The best war monument in the world—Iwo Jima
- The toughest mascot in the world—a bulldog
- The best motivational cry in the world: "Ooh-Rah!"
- Once a Marine, always a Marine

- The concept that every Marine is first and fore most a rifleman
- Everyone is a Marine—officer and enlisted alike
- The Ka-Bar combat knife each Marine carries
- The Marine Corps makes a difference in the world

On a similar note, all Marines feel a profound connection with one another. This deep-seated cohesion arises from a fellowship of shared hardships during times of peace. It also arises from standing shoulder-to-shoulder with their brothers-in-arms to confront dangers in a worthy cause. Marines truly see themselves as proverbial "knights in shining armor" who rush into battle and vanquish Evil, a concept that has been illustrated in several recruiting campaigns. All Marines—past, present, and future—are loyal to one another and to the

Marine Corps, adhering to the motto, *Semper Fidelis*— Always Faithful.

The Marine Corps itself has always recognized that it is not the equipment, technology, or uniform that makes a Marine (although admittedly the Marines' Dress Blues are universally acknowledged as being the sharpest-looking uniform). Rather, it is the man or woman and, more importantly, the spirit within. You see, being a Marine is all about attitude.

Marines are aggressive, and they play to win, doing more with less. They are confident without being cocky, and proud without being arrogant. They are steadfast, but not stubborn. And they work as long and as hard as necessary to get the job done, the words "do or die" vibrating within their souls. No obstacle is insurmountable. None.

Blend all these ingredients together and *esprit de corps* emerges. Granted, it takes time, but that is what boot camp is all about. It is the first step all recruits take to lose their independent civilian nature and, in its place, cloak themselves in the culture, tradition, and mystique of the Marine Corps. If they are strong enough and determined enough, they will eventually earn the title of United States Marine and take their place among the few—the fiercest warrior force this nation owns.

The making of a Marine . . . it all begins at boot camp.

The Iwo Jima Marine Corps Memorial commemorates the raising of the flag atop Mt. Suribachi on February 23, 1945, but it also is dedicated to all Marines who have given their lives in the defense of the United States since 1775. There were actually two flag raisings on Iwo Jima. The famous image captured by AP photographer Joe Rosenthal was the second raising. Both flags were raised by the 3rd Platoon, E Company, 28th Marines.

THE MARINES' HYMN

From the halls of Montezuma
To the shores of Tripoli,
We fight our country's battles
In the air, on land, and sea.
First to fight for right and freedom,
And to keep our honor clean,
We are proud to claim the title
Of United States Marines.

Our flag's unfurl'd to every breeze
From dawn to setting sun;
We have fought in every clime and place
Where we could take a gun.
In the snow of far-off northern lands
And in sunny tropic scenes,
You will find us always on the job—
The United States Marines.

Here's health to you and to our Corps
Which we are proud to serve;
In many a strife we've fought for life
And never lost our nerve.
If the Army and the Navy
Ever gaze on Heaven's scenes,
They will find the streets are guarded
By United States Marines.

FAMOUS MARINES

Don Adams	Actor
James Baker	Secretary of the Treasury and Secretary of State
F. Lee Bailey	Attorney
Gregory Boyington	World War II fighter ace (28 kills) and Medal of Honor recipient, known affectionately as "Pappy" Boyington while with VFM-214 "Black Sheep"
Hugh Brannum	a.k.a. Mr. Green Jeans
Art Buchwald	Newspaper humorist. He enlisted with the Marines before his 17th birthday.
Dale Bumpers	U.S. Senator (Arkansas)
Bugs Bunny	Cartoon character and Honorary Marine during World War II. Was initially given the rank of Private and eventually rose to honorary Sergeant.
John Chaffee	U.S. Senator (Rhode Island) and Secretary of the Navy
Stephen Crane	Author of *The Red Badge of Courage*. He was made an honorary Second Lieutenant by the Marines after participating in the fight at the Battle of Cuzco Well in Cuba in June 1898.
Walter Cunningham	*Apollo 7* astronaut
Edward Dugmore	Abstract-expressionist artist
Glenn Ford	Actor
John H. Glenn	Astronaut and U.S. Senator
Gene Hackman	Actor
Fred Haise	*Apollo 13* astronaut
Charlton Heston	Actor. Was initially given the rank of Private, and eventually rose to honorary Sergeant.
Bob Keeshan	a.k.a. Captain Kangaroo
Fred Lasswell	Cartoonist and creator of *Snuffy Smith*
Jim Lehrer	Television commentator
Jack Lousma	*Columbia* space shuttle commander
Ken MacAfee	Football player
Lee Marvin	Actor
Bob Mathias	Decathlete
Ed McMahon	Sweepstakes spokesperson
Steve McQueen	Actor
J. Richard Munro	Chairman, Time-Warner Inc.
Jim Nabors	Actor who played the dimwitted, but kindly Gomer Pyle on the 1960s television program. He was made an honorary Marine.
Ken Norton	Boxer
George Peppard	Actor
Bum Phillips	Football coach
Tyrone Power	Actor
Dan Rather	Network news anchor
Donald Regan	Secretary of the Treasury
Burt Reynolds	Actor

Charles S. Robb	U.S. Senator (Virginia)	**Lee Trevino**	Golfer
Vincent Sardi	New York restaurateur	**Gene Tunney**	Boxer
George P. Schultz	Secretary of State	**Leon Uris**	Author
George C. Scott	Actor	**Robert Wagner**	Actor
John Philip Sousa	Musician	**John Warner**	U.S. Senator (Virginia)
Leon Spinks Jr.	Boxer	**James Webb**	Secretary of the Navy
Adlai Stevenson III	U.S. Senator (Illinois)	**Ted Williams**	Baseball player
William Styron	Author	**Jonathan Winters**	Comic television star

John H. Glenn Jr., USMC (first row, second from right), was one of the seven original Project Mercury astronauts. *NASA*

TWO

A drill instructor awaits the late-night arrival of recruits at the Receiving Barracks at Parris Island. The design of the building is intended to be stark and intimidating, and the oversized and heavy fortresslike doors—both decorated with the bronze Marine Corps emblem—are a reminder of the serious nature of the training to become a Marine. Inscribed above the doors are the words, "Through these portals pass prospects for America's finest fighting force—United States Marines." They make no promises. After all, not everyone has what it takes to be a Marine. Civilians are not allowed to enter these doors, only Marine recruits. Visitors must enter through a side door. *S. F. Tomajczyk*

The Marine Machine

You earned the title "Marine" upon graduation from boot recruit training. It wasn't willed to you; it isn't a gift. It is not a government subsidy. Few can claim the title; no one can take it away. It is yours forever.
Tom Bartlett,
Leatherneck Magazine

For over 221 years our Corps has done two things for this great Nation. We make Marines, and we win battles.
General Charles C. Krulak,
31st Commandant of the Marine Corps

Dawn never arrives peacefully at Parris Island. Before the sun even begins to peek over the horizon, the air is already filled with the screeches and screams of drill instructors (DIs) who are running, jumping, and dancing in and among the throng of confused and pain-filled recruits, whose sweat steams into the golden light.

"Let's move it! GO! GO! GO!" barks a wild-eyed DI, his spittle spraying into a recruit's ear. "Wazza matter, boot? You got wax in your car? I said, 'MOVE IT!!'"

"Sir, no, sir, this recruit does not have wax in his ear," gulps the young man, standing at rigid attention. "This recruit's legs hurt!"

"Hurt?" says the DI, indifferently. "What, you mean PAIN? Well that's GOOD! Pain is weakness leaving the body."

"But sir . . . "

"BUT? Don't give me any buts." The DI leans closer, both hands on hips, until his face is only an inch from the recruit, and growls, "Did you come here to spoil my beloved Corps?"

"SIR, NO SIR! I did not come here to spoil your beloved Corps, sir!"

"Are you standing up, 'cruit?"

"YES SIR."

"Can you walk?"

"YES SIR."

"THEN WHY ARE YOU WASTING MY TIME?! Sweat dries! Blood clots! Bones heal! Suck it up! Be a Marine! MOVE IT!! GO! GO! GO!" he screams, pointing at the obstacle course. "The only easy day was YESTERDAY!"

Welcome to boot camp.

31

Safely nestled just inside the mouth of Port Royal Sound in the muggy, southern coastal region of South Carolina, Parris Island is distinctly at odds with the nearby luxury resort of Hilton Head Island. While Hilton Head is inundated with golf courses, tennis courts, riding stables, bicycle trails, and marinas, Marine Corps Recruit Depot Parris Island is swarming with "hats" (the nickname given to drill instructors) and is besieged with mosquitoes, alligators, sand fleas, and—at or near the same level of the food chain—"boots," "grapes," and "onion heads"—the lowly recruits who have yet to earn the proud title of Marine.

Encompassing 8,095 acres, of which only 3,262 are habitable (the remaining acres are primarily salt-water marshes), Parris Island is one of two locations in the United States where enlisted Marines undergo basic training. Enlisted Marines have trained at Parris Island since 1915. Male recruits hailing from the eastern United States—and all females—go there, while enlistees west of the Mississippi River go to the Marine Corps Recruit Depot in San Diego. The latter group of individuals have traditionally been referred to as "Hollywood Marines" by many in the Corps, implying that their training is not as rigorous or as miserable as that experienced on the sweltering South Carolina island. After all, how could it be? California is surf, sun, and sand. And Parris Island is . . . well, swamps, spiders, and snakes.

The Marine Corps recognizes that there is a significant difference between the two depots because of climate, facilities, and geography. However, the Corps has taken aggressive steps to ensure that the training process is the same so that "all Marines are created equal." This has been achieved not only by standardizing the concepts, methodology, and philosophy of training, but also by rotating drill instructors, training regiment personnel, and weapons and field training staff between San Diego and Parris Island. As a result, the performance scores and attrition rates for both boot camps are nearly identical.

Regardless of which training depot a recruit attends, the primary purpose of boot camp is to make a

MARINE RECRUITING SLOGANS SINCE 1775

A few good men*
Tell it to the Marines
Let's go! U.S. Marines
An opportunity to see the world
If you want to fight, join the Marines
No one likes to fight, but someone should know how
First to fight
Want action? Join the U.S. Marine Corps.
First in the fight. Always faithful. Be a U.S. Marine.
We don't promise you a rose garden
The Marines are looking for a few good men
The Few. The Proud. The Marines.

* This appeared in the Marine Corps' first recruiting ad in the *Providence Gazette* on March 20, 1779. The ad, written by Marine Captain William Jones, stated: "The Continental ship *Providence*, now lying at Boston, is bound on a short cruise, immediately; a few good men are wanted to make up her complement."

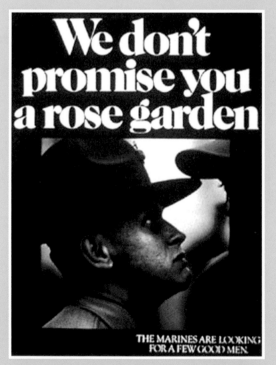

A recruiting poster from the 1970s.

After rushing off the bus and finding a pair of painted footsteps to stand atop of, the frantic recruits stand at attention, hoping to avoid a confrontation with the rabid, screeching drill instructor. On any given day, there are 3,883 male and 537 female recruits at Parris Island. The cost to train one recruit is $14,320. *S. F. Tomajczyk*

To reassure families who may be worrying about their sons and daughters who have gone off to boot camp, the Marine Corps allows each recruit to make a 15-second phone call home. Some have noted that although this appeases the family members, it bears a resemblance to the "one phone call" allowed to a person who has been arrested, only no one is coming to get you—except, of course, a drill instructor. And there are 575 to 600 DIs at Parris Island year-round. *S. F. Tomajczyk*

"basic Marine"—a man or woman who embodies the following traits:

- A warrior spirit
- Basic military knowledge and individual skills
- Discipline, confidence, and self-reliance
- High moral standards
- Physical fitness and wellness as a way of life
- Pride, respect, and love of Corps and country

This does not happen overnight. In fact, it takes the drill instructors at the recruit training battalions 12 weeks to complete this transformation, closely adhering to a time-proven formula that physically and mentally erodes a recruit's civilian influences away and then rebuilds him or her into a Marine. The process is such a dramatic, life-changing event that family members are always shocked by the metamorphosis when they attend the graduation ceremony. The immature, uncertain, and out-of-shape teen they have known since birth has seemingly been supernaturally replaced by a fit, self-assured, and very capable adult Marine warrior.

That change is forever, which is why the Marine Corps embraces the tenet "Once a Marine, always a Marine." Ironically, the evolution from civilian to amphibious Marine—which perhaps only Charles Darwin could truly appreciate—begins "in the pool."

LIFE IN THE POOL

The majority of men and women who enlist in the Marine Corps come directly from high school, having been actively recruited by a local Marine Recruiter. In fact, the average age of a recruit is 19. Every year, the Corps needs to enlist more than 30,000 individuals just to meet the loss of those Marines who retire or do not reenlist, and those recruits who fail to make it through boot camp.

So, within the Marine Corps establishment, the recruiter—like the drill instructor—is held in very high esteem. That is because the recruiting process is an arduous duty: the hours are long and irregular (60–70 hours per week, talking with candidates at night and on weekends); the rejection rate is high from potential recruits (about 95 percent on a daily basis); and the community obligations that come along with the position strain marital relationships, often to the point of divorce. Hence, recruiters have to be self-disciplined, energetic, highly organized, outgoing, and upbeat. They also have to have a spotless military record and an impressive appearance, and be willing to live and work in a civilian world where they cannot hide and where there is little camaraderie with brother Marines.

Marine recruiters have a quota to meet, usually three or four enlistees a month. To find prospects, a recruiter relies on telephone canvassing, recruiting office traffic, and home visits. Nearly all of these efforts are cold calls. To get just one qualified prospect, it is not unusual for a recruiter to have to make as many as 90 calls first. So, to meet his or her quota for the month,

A male recruit receives his 20-second "cranial amputation." Shaving hair off helps eliminate a recruit's individuality and civilian nature. It is among the first things the Marine Corps does to incoming recruits. *S. F. Tomajczyk*

Decked out in identical clothing, the recruits now belong to Uncle Sam or, as some jest, "Uncle Sam's Misguided Children"—a play on the USMC stenciled on their sweatshirts. This photo was taken about 1:00 a.m., and the recruits still had more processing to undergo. *S. F. Tomajczyk*

A RECRUIT'S RIGHTS

According to the "Standard Operating Procedures" of Marine Corps Recruit Depot, Parris Island, ". . . certain rights are fundamental to the welfare of all recruits and shall not be denied." As a result, all recruits have the following rights (with a few exceptions, most notably during the Crucible training phase):
• Eight hours of uninterrupted sleep • One hour of uninterrupted free time daily • A minimum of 20 minutes for each recruit to consume each meal • Attend sick call and follow-up appointments, and use medication prescribed by a medical officer, independent duty corpsman, physician assistant, or nurse practitioner • Attend scheduled religious services and events of their choice in accordance with the Religious Freedom Restoration Act of 1993, and see a chaplain as requested by the recruit • Request mast [i.e., a legal hearing] via the chain-of-command • Make and receive emergency phone calls • Maintain privacy of both incoming and outgoing correspondence without censorship or review • Receive all mail on the day it is received by the parent company • Make emergency head (i.e., bathroom) calls • See visitors

the recruiter must endure the rejection of 270 to 360 calls. This level of rejection becomes difficult to bear day-after-day, month-after-month, for three years.

In addition to basic prospecting, recruiters are also tasked with other daily duties, such as visiting schools and college campuses, and performing at local community events. But perhaps the most demanding duty placed on a recruiter's shoulders is preparing new enlistees for boot camp.

Often referred to as "poolees" in the Marine Corps because they are in the pool of new recruits awaiting their trip to either Parris Island or San Diego, these enlistees are typically brought together at least twice a month (if not weekly) for physical conditioning, academic training, and, on occasion, field trips. The purpose behind all of this is to maintain their enthusiasm and prevent "buyer's remorse" from setting in, while preparing them for the rigors of boot camp, which can be scheduled 3 to 12 months away. The recruiter knows what motivated the recruit to join the Marines in the first place and understands the recruit's background. As a result, the recruiter can remotivate a recruit who is having second thoughts and encourage the recruit to remain in training.

Since attrition rates remain part of a Marine recruiter's permanent military record, it is in his or her best interest to seek out only the best prospects possible and to work closely with them. (This is especially important, given the facts that it costs an average $11,600 to recruit just one person, and that 24 percent of recruits change their mind and bow out before even leaving for boot camp.) As a result, recruiters are on the constant lookout for individuals who have the ability to be transformed into Marines and imbued with its core values of honor, courage, and commitment.

More often than not, these individuals are eagerly sought-after "alphas," young men and women who score in the top 50 percent on the Armed Services Vocational Aptitude Battery (ASVAB). This exam is administered to everyone interested in enlisting in the military. It is structured to determine how much a recruit can learn rather than how much he or she knows. The test results give the military a good idea of the ratings and duties for which a person is best suited. The ASVAB classifies people into five categories, ranging from I to V. Alphas, as already mentioned, score in the top 50 percent (categories I, II, and IIIa). "Bravos" are those who score in the 31–49 percent level, and are also favored by recruiters. Those in

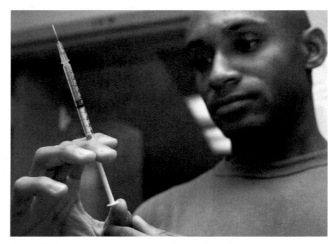

A medical corpsman prepares to give a shot of anthrax vaccine. All Marine recruits receive a number of inoculations during boot camp to protect them from common diseases, as well as from potential biological warfare agents that may be used by enemy forces in combat.

MARINE CORPS OATHS

Enlisted
I do solemnly swear (or affirm) that I will support and defend the Constitution of the United States against all enemies, foreign and domestic; that I will bear true faith and allegiance to the same; that I will obey the orders of the President of the United States and the orders of the officers appointed over me, according to regulations and the Uniform Code of Military Justice.

So help me God.

Officer
I do solemnly swear (or affirm) that I will support and defend the Constitution of the United States against all enemies, foreign and domestic; that I will bear true faith and allegiance to the same; that I take this obligation freely, without any mental reservation or purpose of evasion; and that I will well and faithfully discharge the duties of the office on which I am about to enter.

So help me God.

Three pairs of eyes burn holes through any recruit who dares question an order, makes a mistake, or fails to act quickly enough to satisfy these no-nonsense drill instructors. The campaign hat (a.k.a. "Smokey Bear") is now standard issue for both male and female DIs. Prior to 1996, only male instructors were allowed to wear it. *S. F. Tomajczyk*

Category IV (those who score in the bottom 10–30 percent) are taken only in limited numbers, and Category V (the lowest 9 percent) is not accepted for military service.

SHOCK AND AWE

The Marine Corps intentionally arranges it so recruits arrive at the Marine Corps Recruit Depot, Parris Island, at night. Not only does the darkness impair sensory abilities, but humans have always been anxious about the gloom of night, fearful that something evil is "out there" stalking them. That fear is not lost on the Marine Corps.

In fact, the Corps relies on it to create a stressful atmosphere at boot camp, right from the first minute. They want recruits to be stressed by the fear of the unknown. Later on, the stress comes from fear of failure and the unrelenting demands drill instructors place on them to achieve perfection in all they do. By the end of boot camp, all Marines will have learned how to function in a stressful

environment and how to endure the rigors of military life—important skills when going into combat.

As the bus pulls up to the two-story Receiving Barracks, you can hear nervous laughter, joking, and bravado by the recruits. They think they know what to expect—they've watched television movies, and their recruiter back home gave them some advice—but in the end they haven't a clue. It is always much worse than they ever imagined. And the nightmare begins when a lean, tanned, and impeccably dressed DI—wearing a Smokey-the-Bear field hat tilted at a threatening angle—marches out to the bus without a smile, climbs aboard and then barks a rushing stream of monotone words that translates into something like:

"OnBehalfOfBrigadierGeneralJosephMcMenamin, CommandingGeneralOfTheRecruitDepot,Iwelcome YouToParrisIsland.ThisIsTheReceivingBarracks.YouHave ThirtySecondsToGetYourselfAndYourGearOffThis

BusAndLineUpOnThePaintedFootprintsOnThe Pavement.DoYouUnderstand?"

The recruits give a jumbled response.

"When you are given an order, you will shout, *Yes Sir!* Do you understand?"

"Yes, sir."

The DI cups a hand over his ear. "I CAN'T HEAR YOU! Do you understand?"

"YES SIR!"

"*DO IT!*"

A cascade of bodies pours off the bus. Panic sets in when the recruits cannot find the footprints on the ground, which are (of course) perfectly aligned in columns of three with each pair of prints painted at a precise 45-degree angle. Between the darkness and the orange-tinted light being cast by the artificial streetlights, the yellow footprints are effectively camouflaged. In the background, the DI loudly counts down the time.

"4 . . . 3 . . . 2 . . . 1!"

He immediately pounces on those who have not found their footprints, screaming at them while bouncing up-and-down in apparent rage, frustration, and impatience. No one is moving fast enough for him. No one is yelling, "Yes Sir" loudly enough for him. No is standing at attention rigidly enough for him. Absolutely nothing appeases the drill instructor, and he lets them know it.

The psychological assault has begun. None of the recruits is laughing or joking now. All of them stand in shock and awe. Without a doubt the majority are wondering what the hell they've gotten themselves into. The DI is a madman. Deep inside they just *know* he's crazy and mean enough to kill them.

And that's the way the Marine Corps wants it to be. The DI should be the scariest SOB a recruit ever meets, and the last person he or she ever forgets.

Sweat evaporates off the hot skin of recruits and fills the cool, morning air. As each recruit successfully completes the obstacle course, he quickly falls in line after receiving verbal permission from the drill instructor. Those who fail the course are segregated and given some "incentive" training. Drill instructors wear color-coded shirts to signify the battalion they are affiliated with. In this photo, the red-shirted DI is with the 1st Recruit Training Battalion. *S. F. Tomajczyk*

Above: Oops! Ideally, you want to be on top of the rope, not below it. Having to support one's entire body weight with arms and legs quickly tires a recruit, and he (or she) is destined to fall off. A number of recruits make this error early on in boot camp. Safety nets are strung beneath some confidence-course obstacles, and water pits for others. So if you see a dripping-wet recruit, it's a clue to what happened. *S. F. Tomajczyk*

Left: The sun peeks over the horizon at Parris Island, but the recruits have been undergoing training for several hours now. "Boots" who are nursing an injury back to health serve as gear guards. They watch over the packs and equipment of the other Marines as they train. While theft is nonexistent—no Marine *ever* steals—this practice is intended to build the recruits' trust and reliance on one another. In battle, they will need that faith. *S. F. Tomajczyk*

Right: Hovering over a recruit like a hawk waiting to pounce on prey, this DI urges the "boot" over the wall obstacle. The voice of a DI is extremely distinctive and froggy—the result of so much yelling that the vocal cords are permanently damaged. But the tone is motivating, penetrating the fog filling a recruit's head. DIs routinely lament that most of today's recruits are overweight, lack upper body strength, and are "Nintendo heads." The majority of recruits who are dropped or discharged from training fall out during the first three weeks. *S. F. Tomajczyk*

Soon the recruits are all at attention, and standing in neat formation—but only because of the footprints. The women are separated from the men, and then both groups are marched into the barracks, where a pack of equally deranged and rabid DIs awaits them. The building reverberates with screams and shouts, and of confused recruits scrambling to follow orders, often bumping into one another. (And woe to the "boot" who accidentally slams into a DI!)

This is Processing, and it is where recruits leave the world behind. After making a 15-second phone call home ("I've arrived safely. Do not send me food or bulky items. I will let you know my mailing address later."), the recruits find themselves sitting in a large classroom where a DI has them throw away personal items considered to be contraband. This includes: tobacco products, food, chewing gum, over-the-counter medications, vitamins, alcohol, lighters, pornographic materials, weapons, knives with a blade longer than 3 inches, cards, dice, cologne, toothpaste, and shampoo.

Next, prohibited items are seized, placed inside a brown bag, and then sealed and stored away until the recruit graduates from boot camp. This includes athletic equipment (except running shoes), civilian clothes (females are allowed to keep bras and underwear), cameras, radios, cell phones, photographs larger than wallet size, knives, and birth control devices (an exception is made for birth control pills for women). All medications are evaluated by medical personnel to ensure that the recruit is not being treated for an undisclosed medical condition that could result in a discharge from the military.

After a quick physical examination and some necessary paperwork, each male recruit gets a 30-second "cranial amputation," the infamous shaved scalp that erases his outward individuality. Until Training Day 48 (TD-48), all men will continue to get buzz cuts. After that time, they are permitted to sport a "high and tight" haircut—short on the sides with a wee bit of hair on top.

Women are spared the "onion head," "bubblehead," and "grape" look, but they must keep their hair shorter

than collar length. Faddish hairstyles are forbidden, as are ponytails and unbalanced haircuts. For women who sported longer hair in the civilian world, trimming it can be just as traumatic as a male being shaved.

By now, it's after midnight. Over the next several hours the 'cruits will receive their military clothing, sea bag, boots, athletic gear, and other items. If they're fortunate, they will get one or two hour's sleep before reveille at 0500 hours.

Over the next three days, the Marine Corps receiving staff begin indoctrinating the recruits to military life. At this point, neither the men nor the women have left the Receiving Barracks, and they have not yet been assigned to a training company. They are essentially isolated from the world. That, too, like everything the Marine Corps does, is intentional. It is part of the tearing down process. Recruits must be purged of all civilian patterns of behavior. Individuality must be replaced with teamwork and unity.

BOOT CAMP HIGHLIGHTS

Phase I

Week 1: General Military Skills• First 1.5-mile run• Marine Corps Martial Arts Program• Bayonet Techniques• Customs and Courtesies• Core Values Classes• USMC History Course• Introduction to the M16A2 Service Rifle

Week 2: General Military Skills• First Aid Classes• Pugil Sticks I• Physical Training• Weapons Handling Classes• Throws and Falls• USMC History and Terrorism Awareness Courses• Circuit Course• Inoculations

Week 3: General Military Skills• Pugil Sticks II• Confidence Course• 3-Mile Conditioning March• Counters to Strikes• USMC Leadership History Course• Uniform Code of Military Justice Course

Week 4: General Military Skills• Senior Drill Instructor Inspection• Series Commander Inspection• Initial Drill Evaluation• MCMAP Testing• Pugil Sticks III

Phase II

Week 5: Swim Week• Combat Survival Swimming• MCMAP Testing• 5-Mile Conditioning March

Week 6: Grass Week• Introduction to Marksmanship• Fundamentals of Marksmanship• 35-Yard Grouping• Endurance Course• Field Meet

Week 7: Firing Week• Known Distance Firing• M16A2 Rifle Qualification• Confidence Course• 6-Mile Conditioning March• Small Unit Leadership

Week 8: Team Week•Obstacle Course• 10-Mile Conditioning March

Phase III

Week 9: Field Training •A-Line (Firing Range)• Fundamentals of Field Firing• Unknown Distance Firing• Multiple Target Engagement• Limited Exposure Exercise• Moving Targets• Daylight Target Detection• Night Firing• NBC Mask Firing• Academic Review

Week 10: Basic Warrior Training• Combat Endurance Course• Basic Field Skills• Gas Chamber• Final Drill Competition• Final Physical Training Test• Rappelling Tower• NBC Training• Company Commander's Inspection• Final Drill• Practical Application Testing • Defensive Driving Course• Land Navigation• Military Operations in Urban Terrain (MOUT) Movement Course• Day/Night Individual Movement

Week 11: The Crucible• 54-Hour Crucible Event• Warrior's Breakfast• Once a Marine, Always a Marine• Core Values• Recruit Liberty

Week 12: Graduation• Battalion Commander's Inspection• Financial Responsibility Course• Motivational Run• Marine Corps Emblem Ceremony• Family Day• Graduation

A DI from the 4th Recruit Training Battalion, the only battalion that trains female Marine recruits, tries to understand why this particular recruit is having such a difficult time climbing a rope. To her, it seems so easy. After giving another demonstration, which does not solve anything, the frustrated DI orders the recruit to begin the obstacle course all over again. Would-be Marines have some important lessons to heed: Do your best, no matter how trivial the task. Pursue excellence. Look out for the group before you look out for yourself. And don't whine or make excuses. *S. F. Tomajczyk*

Orders must be followed immediately, and without question. Authority must be respected.

The Marine Corps forbids the use of profanity, hazing, verbal abuse, and physical contact against recruits (exceptions to physical contact are if it corrects a recruit's position, adjusts the arrangement of clothing or equipment, prevents injury, provides first aid, or is used in self-defense from assault). The Corps also forbids using racially or ethnically degrading language to address a recruit, including the demeaning terms "canary" and "alligator." They are to be addressed by last name, grade (e.g., private), billet (e.g., cook), or as "recruit."

However, the Marine Corps does allow raised voices and the constant demand by drill instructors for excellence. As a result, every glance, twitch, false step, uttered word, and gasp a recruit makes invites an immediate verbal cuffing from a drill instructor.

In instances where discipline and motivation need to be instilled, or a minor disciplinary infraction needs to be corrected, DIs resort to incentive training (IT)—or as the recruits refer to it, "intensive torture." It is a combination of three exercises selected from a list of a dozen

Walking up a wall is easy, if you remember to keep your body at the correct angle and walk foot-over-foot, hand-over-hand. This recruit obviously has it down pat. But for many others, the wall will remain a blister-filled challenge for several weeks until they finally master it. The average recruit's upper body strength improves dramatically during boot camp. This is true for both men and women. *S. F. Tomajczyk*

Above: A bayonet is essentially a knife at the end of a pole, which enables a Marine to strike, wound, or kill an opponent at a relatively safe distance. Marine recruits learn five offensive techniques with the bayonet and rifle: straight thrust, slash, horizontal buttstroke, vertical buttstroke, and the smash. Every attack is to be ruthless, with the Marine getting his blade into the enemy as quickly as possible—preferably in the throat, stomach, or face. *S. F. Tomajczyk*

Left: When a recruit reaches the top of the rope, he yells out his name and platoon number, along with "I see Jesus, Sir!" Then he asks permission to climb back down. If any candidate fails to do this, he is likely to be sent back to the beginning of the obstacle course for a repeat performance. All exercises and drills end with the cry "Marine Corps!" It is repeated hundreds of times a day, psychologically reinforcing their affiliation with the few and the proud. *S. F. Tomajczyk*

that are performed for six to eight minutes (depending on how far advanced the recruits are in the 12-week training schedule), with a 30-second break midway through. Some of the more painful (and hated) exercises have nicknames like "steam engines," "mountain climbers," and "crunches." Due to the complexity of the rules governing IT—when it is appropriate, where it can be carried out, what exceptions forbid it, how many repetitions of each exercise can be administered—drill

Above: Recruits learn hand-to-hand combat fighting techniques as part of the new Marine Corps Martial Arts Program. Referred to by many as "Semper Fu," it is taught to recruits at Parris Island at a facility called Thunderdome, an open-air shelter that has a 7-inch-thick base of wood chips to soften the falls of recruits and prevent injury. All Marines are required to have at least a tan belt in MCMAP—even the Commandant of the Marine Corps. As of this writing, General Michael Hagee holds a gray belt in the martial arts program, the next degree of skill above tan belt. *S. F. Tomajczyk*

Right: A recruit shouts the standard "Aye, aye, sir!" as a drill instructor hustles the recruits back into the squad bay at Marine Corps Recruit Depot San Diego. There is no individuality in the Marine Corps, at least during boot camp. As a result, recruits are forbidden from using the word "I." Instead they must always speak in the third person (e.g., "This recruit would like to . . ..").

instructors are required to carry the *Recruit Training Pocket Guide* at all times during work hours so they can refer to it.

While in processing, recruits undergo a thorough physical and dental examination, including urinalysis testing and blood testing for HIV. If a recruit has an allergy or condition that could be life-threatening, he or she is issued three medical alert tags, one of which is laced into the right tennis shoe and each right boot.

An initial strength test (IST) is administered to determine whether or not a recruit is at a level of physical fitness to actually begin training. The Corps knows boot camp is physically taxing, and does not want recruits ending up in the hospital. Each male recruit must meet the following minimum standards: two pull-ups from a dead hang, 44 crunches in two minutes, and a 1.5-mile run in 13 minutes and 30 seconds. Females must do a 12-second flexed arm hang, 44 crunches in two minutes and a 1.5-mile run in 15 minutes.

As is evident from this, the Marines expect female recruits to come close to matching the demands placed on males. As far as the Marine Corps is concerned, all Marines are equal.

Those who fail the initial strength test are sent to a physical conditioning platoon for some serious exercising, dieting, and weight training until they pass the IST. Overweight recruits are placed on an 1,800-calorie diet; underweight recruits, 4,500 calories. As soon as they pass the standards, they are returned to regular training.

Physical and medical issues aside, recruits also receive schooling in basic military knowledge during processing. This includes instruction on general orders, Marine and Navy rank structure, chain of command, naval terminology, Uniform Code of Military Justice, and weapons safety rules. They learn how to salute, how to stand interior guard, how to break in boots, and how to avoid heat and cold-weather injuries. At this time, they are issued an unloaded M16A2 5.56mm service rifle and receive an overview on proper handling procedures. More in-depth training on the rifle is forthcoming in Week One of boot camp and beyond. Until then, they carry the rifle everywhere they go, so it becomes a natural extension of them.

Processing is a hectic three days and, although the recruits find it stressful, it is nothing compared to what they are about to endure. In a process known as "forming," the receiving drill instructors finally march the recruits to their assigned platoons (70–80 recruits each) at a recruit training battalion, which serves as their home for the

Although women are prohibited from combat duty, they do assume roles and responsibilities in war that could easily bring them into harm's way. This is one of the reasons the Marine Corps trains female Marines in the same tactics and techniques as the men. The Corps understands that if a position is attacked, it is better if everyone knows marksmanship and combat tactics to rebuff enemy forces.
S. F. Tomajczyk

Pugil-stick fighting essentially allows recruits to conduct real-world bayonet fighting without the bayonet. The black-colored end of the pugil stick represents the butt of the rifle; the red end, the bayonet. Recruits wear protective gear (including helmet, groin padding, chest padding, and a mouthpiece) to avoid serious injury. Two DIs serve as referees and immediately end the bout when what is perceived to be a lethal blow has been delivered—such as a head strike. Pugil stick bouts are as exciting as any modern sport, and it is typical for recruits and DIs on the sideline to cheer their favorites. *S. F. Tomajczyk*

The Marine Corps is not only a "band of brothers," but it is also a "band of sisters." The first female Marine was Opha M. Johnson, who enlisted in 1918 as a "Marinette." Today, roughly six percent of the Marine Corps is female—about 9,500 enlisted and 1,000 officers. *S. F. Tomajczyk*

One of the mantras of the Marine Corps is: Every Marine a rifleman. Marksmanship is vitally important to the Corps because, since it is often the first military service to arrive on scene and fight, everyone sent is guaranteed to spend time behind a rifle. Hence, the better every Marine shoots, the more quickly a conflict can be ended. Intense and lethal gunfire can demoralize the largest of armies. *S. F. Tomajczyk*

next 12 weeks. Parris Island has four such battalions, and each is identified by a unique T-shirt color scheme worn by its training staff:

> 1st Recruit Training Battalion—Red
> 2nd Recruit Training Battalion—Yellow
> 3rd Recruit Training Battalion—Blue
> 4th Recruit Training Battalion—Burgundy*

In a precise, ceremonial fashion, the company commander, series commander, and the senior drill instructor (SDI) greet the recruits in the squad bay with standard presentations. The series commander, who is usually a captain with a gunnery sergeant (E-7) as the senior NCO, introduces the recruits to their drill instructors, who publicly reaffirm their commitment to making them into

United States Marines by reciting the DI Pledge, which was written in 1956:

> "These recruits are entrusted to my care. I will train them to the best of my ability. I will develop them into smartly disciplined, physically fit, basically trained Marines, thoroughly indoctrinated in love of Corps and country. I will demand of them and demonstrate by my own example, the highest standards of personal conduct, morality, and professional skill."

Three drill instructors ("hats" in Marine parlance) are assigned to the platoon. The senior drill instructor, who is usually a staff sergeant (E-6), is known as the "black belt,"

* This battalion is strictly for female recruits

A Marine recruit who is firing his M16 5.56mm service rifle at a target at an unknown distance, reaches back into his ammo pouch for another 30-round magazine. The green smoke swirling on the field screens the Marine's line of sight, making it more difficult to hit the target. The training prepares him for the obscurants that may be deployed on a future battlefield. Recruits spend a week "on the grass" learning the four firing positions: prone, sitting, kneeling, and standing. Getting into a firing position is often painful, since you end up using muscles you didn't realize you had. *S. F. Tomajczyk*

"THIS IS MY RIFLE"
THE CREED OF A UNITED STATES MARINE

This creed was written by Major General William H. Rupertus, USMC (1889–1945), who was the commanding general of Marine Corps Base, San Diego, in the early years of World War II. He was concerned that the newly trained Marines understand "that the only weapon which stands between them and death is the rifle. . . . They must understand that their rifle is their life. . . . It must become a creed with them." He jotted down his thoughts on a scrap of paper and had Captain Robert P. White, USMCR, public relations officer of the base, edit it. The creed, "My Rifle," is still taught to all Marines undergoing basic training. It was first published in the San Diego *Marine Corps Chevron* on March, 14, 1942.

This is my rifle. There are many like it, but this one is mine.

My rifle is my best friend. It is my life. I must master it as I master my life.

My rifle, without me, is useless. Without my rifle, I am useless. I must fire my rifle true. I must shoot straighter than any enemy who is trying to kill me. I must shoot him before he shoots me. I will.

My rifle and myself know that what counts in this war is not the rounds we fire, the noise of our burst, nor the smoke we make. We know that it is the hits that count. We will hit.

My rifle is human, even as I, because it is my life. Thus, I will learn it as a brother. I will learn its weakness, its strength, its parts, its accessories, its sights, and its barrel. I will keep my rifle clean and ready, even as I am clean and ready. We will become part of each other. We will.

Before God I swear this creed. My rifle and myself are the defenders of my country. We are the masters of our enemy. We are the saviors of my life.

So be it, until victory is America's and there is no enemy, but Peace!

since he or she wears a glossy, black patent-leather belt about the waist as a symbol of authority. (The terms "Top" and "Big Dad" are also used.) The senior DI assumes the role of mentor to the recruits—a parental and nurturing individual who has a voice of reason. All take an instant liking to their black belt. By contrast, the two "green

Left: With the growing possibility of having to fight in an environment contaminated with chemical or biological warfare agents, the Marine Corps is ensuring all recruits receive training on how to accurately fire their weapons while wearing a gas mask. The masks are hot and stuffy, they restrict peripheral vision, and the eye-pieces can fog up (as this photo demonstrates). This "train as you fight" concept is deeply embedded in the Corps. *S. F. Tomajczyk*

Below: Recruits negotiate the Day Movement Course at Camp Pendleton, California. The course simulates a combat environment with pneumatic machine-gun fire, artillery-explosion simulators, and a variety of obstacles, including barbed wire. The recruits are expected to put to use the individual movement techniques they have learned so far, such as the tactical low- and high-crawls.

belts"—so named for the green, web belts worn about their waists—are universally despised. The second-in-command (second hat) is referred to as "the heavy" and is largely responsible for the recruits' instruction. The third-in-command (third hat) is known as "killer" because of the disciplinarian role he or she plays.

Together, in a sort of "good cop, bad cop" manner, these three drill instructors are responsible for turning flabby, weak-minded civilians into determined, rock-hard Marines. After introducing the assistant DIs, the black belt makes the following speech to the recruits, reinforcing what is expected of them in the upcoming weeks of training:

"Our mission is to train each one of you to become a United States Marine.

"A Marine is characterized as one who possesses the highest military virtues. He/she obeys orders, respects his/her seniors, and strives constantly to be the best in everything he/she does. Discipline and spirit are the hallmarks of a Marine. Each of you can become a Marine if you develop discipline and spirit. We will give every effort to train you, even after some of you have given up on yourselves.

"Starting now, you will treat me and all other Marines with the highest respect, for we have earned our place as Marines and will accept nothing less than that from you. We will treat you as we do our fellow Marines, with firmness, fairness, dignity, and compassion.

"At no time will you be physically or verbally abused by any Marine or recruit. If anyone should abuse or mistreat you, I expect you to report such incidents immediately to me or one of my drill instructors. Further, if you believe that I have mistreated you, I expect you to report it to the series commander. My drill instructors and I will be with you every day, everywhere you go.

Throughout the 12 weeks of boot camp, recruits march and drill, march and drill, and then march and drill some more. Doing so builds teamwork and prepares them for unit tactical movements in the field later on. As they drill, their DI keeps a sharp eye out for sloppiness. As much as the recruits are evaluated on their drilling performance, so too is the DI. At the platoon's final drill competition, the DI will be handed a card outlining the drills he is to lead the platoon through. As a sergeant of Marines, he is graded on how well he has trained his recruits to crisply execute orders. *S. F. Tomajczyk*

A group of candidates to become Drill Instructors lines up to enter the gas chamber, where they will be exposed to high levels of CS, the military's designation for tear gas. Once inside the sealed building, CS crystals will be dispensed and the Marines will undergo a series of maneuvers to test their ability to safely remove and put back on their gas masks. If they fail to do it properly, they will suffer the consequences of the tear gas. The top careers within the Marine Corps—besides infantryman—are Drill Instructor and Marine Security Guard. *S. F. Tomajczyk*

"I have told you what my drill instructors and I will do. From you we expect the following:
- You **must** give 100 percent of yourself at all times.
- Obey **all** orders, quickly, willingly, and without question.
- Treat **all** Marines and recruits with courtesy and respect.
- You **will not** physically abuse or verbally threaten another Marine or recruit.
- Be completely honest in everything you do. A Marine **never** lies, cheats, or compromises.
- Respect the rights and property of all others. A Marine **never** steals.
- You **must** work hard to strengthen your body.
- Be proud of yourself and the uniform you wear.
- Try your best to learn the things you will be taught.
- Above all else, **never** quit or give up!

"We offer you the challenge of recruit training—the opportunity to earn the title United States Marine!"

Left: Before moving through the scrubby South Carolina woods on a simulated combat patrol mission, the DI sketches out the formation he wants the recruits to follow. On the battlefield, Marines must move and fight in formations that allow them to quickly disperse and shoot at the enemy without hitting their comrades. Among the many combat formations the recruits learn are the column, wedge, skirmishers right or left, echelon right or left, and squad vee. *S. F. Tomajczyk*

The tear gas agent CS, which is used primarily for riot control, causes lacrymation, choking, and shortness of breath. As this photo clearly demonstrates, it has a painful and dramatic effect on the Marines who were exposed to it in the gas chamber. To remove traces of the gas from their clothing and gear, the Marines walk several times in a circle with their arms outstretched. Then, after removing the air filter, they douse their gas masks in water. *S. F. Tomajczyk*

There are many ways to cross a river or chasm, including the use of rope. In this photo, recruits learn how to use two ropes to cross a simulated obstacle. It is more difficult than it looks because both ropes move—often in different directions. Furthermore, the bottom rope bounces up and down as recruits of varying weights move across the rope. The technique is made even more difficult when the recruits are tasked with transporting several 50-pound ammo boxes across the rope bridge. *S. F. Tomajczyk*

"If you're not sucking and swallowing sand, you're not doing it right." That is the advice DIs give with regard to doing the low crawl. Moving forward on elbows and kneecaps while keeping the lowest profile possible, a Marine recruit carries his rifle palms-up in front of him to keep sand out of the breech. This is a painful and slow way to advance on the battlefield, but it beats biting a bullet. *S. F. Tomajczyk*

Military commanders use patrols to gather information about the enemy, the ground the Marines are fighting on, and the friendly troops near them. As a patrol moves slowly and deliberately through the terrain, they use concealment to protect them from being observed by enemy forces. This includes remaining motionless while observing, staying in the shadows, blending in with the background, and—as the two Marine recruits in this photo demonstrate—keeping a low profile. *S. F. Tomajczyk*

In the movie *The Patriot*, Mel Gibson as French and Indian War hero Benjamin Martin tells his children, "Aim small, miss small." Marines take this advice to heart by being as small a target as possible on the battlefield. They seek cover behind trees, rocks, and stumps, and hide in culverts, artillery holes, and dug entrenchments. To paraphrase General Patton, in battle, the idea is to get the other bastard to give up his life for his country while you keep yours. *S. F. Tomajczyk*

HELL ON EARTH

The Marine Corps firmly believes that the more one sweats in peace, the more the enemy bleeds in war. At Parris Island, sweat is everywhere. Recruits sweat. DIs sweat. Even the sand fleas, which are forever drilling into recruits, sweat. ("Did you just flick a Marine sand flea off you?" screams a drill instructor. "Let my bugs eat!")

The boot camp training cycle is divided into three distinct phases: Phase I (weeks 1–4) focuses on physical conditioning, close-order drilling, and self-defense. Phase II (weeks 5–8) provides instruction on combat water survival and weapons marksmanship. Phase III (weeks 9–12) teaches basic warrior skills, such as rappelling, low-light shooting, and target acquisition. Throughout all phases, recruits receive a total of 279.5 hours of academic study in general military subjects (such as troop formations, leadership, close combat), drill and ceremonies (including close order drill, manual of arms, parades), and marksmanship and field training (fast-rope, multiple target engagement, and nuclear, biological, and chemical warfare, for example).

Each day begins with reveille at 0500 hours (5:00 a.m.) and is followed after breakfast by morning PT, which usually comprises the "Daily 16" (a series of stretching exercises and calisthenics), formation runs, and, on some days, running through the obstacle course or confidence course. High-risk recruits—those who are overweight, those who failed the IST, or those who have had previous heat and cold injuries—are clearly identified to the drill instructors by two white or red horizontal bars painted on their sweatshirts. The DIs keep a close eye on them, especially during summer days, because they are extremely susceptible to heat stroke.

Following PT, the rest of the day is filled with hours of instruction, drilling, academic courses, squad bay cleaning and maintenance, and meals. A DI conducts a hygiene inspection of each recruit on a daily basis. Standing in underwear, recruits are closely checked for clean fingernails and toenails, clean teeth, clean ears, clear eyes, blisters, ticks, undressed wounds, abnormal bruising, breathing problems, and other physical ailments. One of the more serious medical conditions that can develop is cellulitis, a condition of inflammation of the skin characterized by redness, warmth, swelling, and tenderness. If not treated early and properly, complications may arise, such as abscesses, tissue destruction, or bone infections.

Recruits have Sundays off, but since they are not permitted to go off base or to use many of the on-base facilities, they do not have much to do except sleep, study, wash clothes, and write letters. If they do go out, they are never allowed to be alone. The Marine Corps is all about unity and teamwork. There is no such thing as "individual," so each is accompanied by a buddy everywhere he or she goes.

One thing a recruit quickly learns is that a considerable amount of time is spent marching and drilling. Drills accustom a recruit to working as a member of a team—a team that, in fact, is moving together in unison and to a measured cadence. The purposes of drills are to:
- Move a unit from one place to another in an orderly manner
- Teach discipline
- Develop team spirit
- Provide formations from which combat formations can be quickly assumed

The Marine Corps recently introduced a new line of camouflaged clothing featuring this computer-generated, digital "pixel pattern." If you look at other photos in this book, you'll see how successful this design is at blending Marines in with many different types of environments. The new "camies" also present ergonomic pockets: they are slanted to allow quick-and-easy access. *S. F. Tomajczyk*

In the beginning, recruits are sloppy at drill work and severely test the patience of the drill instructors. They don't align in a straight line. The spacing between individuals is uneven. Their pace is off. And so the DIs rely on repetitive training for hours on end to ingrain proper habits. At some point—usually by Phase II—it finally clicks and everything comes together. The recruits march with precise 30-inch strides. Their arms swing easily in a natural arc, 6 inches straight to the front and 3 inches to the rear. They move confidently, precisely, and automatically to orders.

NONCOMMISSIONED OFFICER'S CREED

I am the backbone of the United States Marine Corps, I am a Marine Noncommissioned Officer.

I serve as part of the vital link between my commander (and all officers) and enlisted Marines. I will never forget who I am or what I represent.

I will challenge myself to the limit and be ever attentive to duty. I am now, more than ever, committed to excellence in all that I do, so that I can set the proper example for other Marines.

I will demand of myself all the energy, knowledge, and skills I possess, so that I can instill confidence in those I teach. I will constantly strive to perfect my own skills and to become a good leader.

Above all, I will be truthful in all I say or do. My integrity shall be impeccable as my appearance. I will be honest with myself, with those under my charge, and with my superiors.

I pledge to do my best to incorporate all the leadership traits into my character. For such is the heritage I have received from that long, illustrious line of professionals who have worn the bloodstripe so proudly before me. I must give the very best I have for my Marines, my Corps, and my Country, for though today I instruct and supervise in peace, tomorrow, I may lead in war.

When marching, the DIs often chant a sing-song cadence (a.k.a. Jody call) to keep the recruits in rhythm. Cadences can be serious, humorous, and, in many instances, downright crass. Some of the better known are "Tarzan and Jane" and "I Can Run to Iraq." After the drill instructor bellows out a line, all the recruits just as loudly echo the words.

An example of a cadence is:

Navy, Navy, I'm in doubt,
Boy your bellies are sticking out!
Is it whiskey, or is it wine?
Or is it lack of PT time?

And, from "They Want to Wear the Red and Gold":

In the Army, young and old
They wanna wear our Red and Gold.
A thousand men will arrive today,
I hear they all were Green Berets!

In addition to normal marches and drills, the recruits are subjected to so-called "conditioning" marches. In the first 47 training days, they undertake four of these marches, each longer than the previous. They cover 3, 5, 6, and 10 miles in distance. The purpose of the conditioning marches is to prepare the recruits for the Crucible during Week 11, in which they will march nearly 40 miles wearing combat gear.

The conditioning marches are conducted at a speed of 3 miles per hour during daylight, and 2.5 miles per hour at night to preserve unit integrity, prevent running, and maintain responsiveness. The DIs are forbidden to physically push, shove, drag, or carry a recruit to keep up with or finish a march.

The conditioning marches are always accompanied by two safety vehicles, each staffed by a corpsman and equipped with one stretcher and two coolers of ice water. In the sizzling summer months, the marches are begun early in the morning to minimize the impact of the heat on the recruits.

NO PAIN, NO GAIN

Boot camp is a progressive process. In the beginning, it tears down a recruit both mentally and physically, and then it purposely rebuilds the recruit by instilling confidence and competence. The Marine Corps shows recruits

To pass through a barbed-wire obstacle without getting snagged, Marine recruits lie on their backs and use the length of their rifles to safely lift the wire high enough for them to wiggle underneath. *S. F. Tomajczyk*

that they can do more than they ever thought they could, simply by taking them to the breaking point, and then beyond. Every training day and every event builds on the previous ones. By the end of the boot camp, the recruits have the mental toughness, poise, and skills that make them Marines.

Among all the training areas a recruit is exposed to during boot camp, four strongly influence this outcome.

MARINE CORPS MARTIAL ARTS PROGRAM (MCMAP)

Known as "Mick-Map," "Semper Fu," and "Fu-Rah!" by recruits, this martial arts program was introduced in 2001 by then-Commandant General James L. Jones to replace the LINE system of defensive close-combat fighting. Jones set a deadline of October 2003 for all Marines (regardless of age, rank, or length of service) to earn a tan belt in MCMAP. That goal was successfully reached, and it subsequently made the Marine Corps America's only armed service in which every member is a skilled martial arts practitioner.

The program, which is more offensive in nature than LINE, blends several Asian martial arts systems (including kung fu, karate, jujitsu, and judo) with bayonet and knife fighting techniques so that Marines can conduct hand-to-hand combat using kicks, throws, punches, falls, choke holds, joint manipulations, grappling, and defensive maneuvers. MCMAP is a progressive, weapons-based program in that a Marine learns to fight with fists, then with a "rifle" (using pugil sticks in training), and followed afterward with knife techniques. This concept has given rise to a new philosophy—One Mind. Any Weapon.—a credo that is stenciled on the sweatshirts of all MCMAP instructors.

By undergoing this martial arts training, Marines become more physically fit and mentally prepared for combat situations. All recruits at boot camp—male and female alike—begin MCMAP on Training Day 1 (TD-1) and receive 27.5 hours of instruction to qualify them for tan belt. Hand-to-hand techniques aside, they learn how to fight under combat conditions, training in such areas as moving over rough terrain, closing and engaging the enemy, fighting while fatigued, and making sound judgments in the heat of battle.

The program encompasses much more than fighting skills; it also embraces leadership, conduct, safety, continuum of force, and rules of engagement. In the end, it is largely responsible for the change in a recruit's attitude and character during boot camp. (In fact, many recruits proudly cheer: "U.S. Marine Corps—100 percent Whoop Ass!")

MCMAP is considered to be such an important training area that if a recruit fails the test on Training Day 22 (TD-22), he or she is recycled through training up to three more times. After failing the test a fourth time, the recruit is considered for separation from the Marine Corps.

Marines receive ongoing MCMAP training throughout their military career, and can earn the right to wear a progression of different colored belts, including gray (46 additional hours of training), green (55 hours), brown (65 hours), and six degrees of black (71.5 hours for first degree).

WATER SURVIVAL

The amphibious nature of a U.S. Marine is to serve near water, whether it is an ocean, lake, river, or swamp. As a result, Marines habitually face a variety of potential water emergencies: ships, watercraft, and amphibious assault vehicles can sink; aircraft can crash; and Marines can accidentally fall into the water. The Corps recognizes this danger and provides all recruits with a Combat Water Survival course, which is taught during Week 5 at boot camp.

Although a surprising number of Marine recruits do not know how to swim, the water survival course is specifically designed to teach them how to remain afloat. There are four levels of swimmer qualification, each more stringent that its predecessor. Every recruit must pass Combat Water Survival Class 4 (CWS-4)—the minimum level of ability—to remain in the Marine Corps. Some specialties, such as aviation, require a higher minimum standard.

Over the span of five days, the recruits are introduced to a number of techniques that will keep them

A martial arts instructor (black shirt with the saying "One Mind. Any Weapon." stenciled on it) demonstrates how to thrust a knife into an enemy from the front to cause as much internal-organ damage as possible. In the upward stroke, the knife blade will hit portions of the kidney, stomach, lungs, and, if the thrust is deep enough and doesn't deflect off the rib cage, the heart. The Marine Corps' Ka-Bar knife has a 7-inch blade—perfectly designed for hand-to-hand combat. *S. F. Tomajczyk*

When the air is filled with lead and you dare not lift your head even a fraction of an inch, hug the earth. To present the smallest possible target to the enemy (and to shrapnel from exploding artillery shells and grenades), Marine recruits are taught to lie flat and turn their heads sideways. By slinging the rifle over their forearm by its sling, they are still able to wiggle forward to safety without getting dirt and sand in the breech or barrel. *S. F. Tomajczyk*

Since the Marines operate on, in, or near the water, the danger of drowning is a real one. As part of their water-survival course, Marine recruits learn to float in deep water while wearing their combat gear. By leaning one's head back in the water and firmly pressing it against the pack, the head will remain above water—admittedly not by much, as this photo demonstrates, but enough to breathe. The key to this survival technique is not to panic. If you do, you risk swallowing water and possibly drowning. Fortunately for the recruits, lifeguards are spaced around the pool during training. Although recruits are not forced into the water against their will, failure to do so can mean a discharge from the Marines. *S. F. Tomajczyk*

alive on the high seas. One of the things they learn is that a correctly packed combat backpack—regardless of its weight—will actually assist them in staying afloat, rather than cause them to sink like a stone to Davy Jones' locker. Another thing they learn is that utility trousers can be used as a floatation device if they are tied off and inflated with air. And still yet another secret is that by reclining in the water—and resting against their combat pack—they can pedal their legs like a bicycle and slowly move forward, their head just barely sticking above water.

The recruits also learn how to properly abandon ship. Wearing combat gear, they walk off 5- and 10-foot-high towers into the pool. As they do so, they cross their arms across their chests, keep their eyes forward, and then cross their legs as they plummet into the water below. (While the exercise is helpful, it does not really prepare the recruits for a 30-foot drop from a naval warship, or a 90-foot drop from an aircraft carrier's flight

deck. In those instances, for example, helmets must be removed, otherwise the Marines risk snapping their necks upon impact with the water.)

Throughout the training, instructors line the side of the pool, keeping an eye out for signs of distress. This includes a swimmer motioning or asking for help, ceasing all forward motion, ingesting water and failing to spit it out, or no longer being able to continue. When trouble rears its ugly head, the instructors immediately toss out a red buoy and haul the recruit poolside.

In the unlikely event a life-threatening situation occurs—a recruit is choking on water for instance—a "Red Dog" alert is sounded. Instructors yell out the phrase and hit one of four red emergency buttons on either side of the pool, sounding a buzzer. Everyone is immediately evacuated from the pool as the endangered recruit is pulled from the water and given basic life support until the first responders arrive.

A squad patrols the abandoned airfield on Parris Island during the Crucible. While it may seem the Marine recruits are too scattered to present a cohesive fighting force in the event an enemy appears, the dispersion is intentional. In combat, space saves lives. It is nearly impossible for a bomb, grenade, or machine gunner to wipe out the entire squad if they are widely spaced out. *S. F. Tomajczyk*

Fighting in an urban environment brings a lot of new and challenging requirements. For instance, a Marine now has to worry about enemy forces located not only at street level, but also in multistory buildings, as well as on roofs, in basements, and in sewer systems. When attacking a building, Marines must first isolate it, then enter the structure and, finally, methodically clear the building room by room and floor by floor. It is a slow, tedious, and adrenaline-draining process. *S. F. Tomajczyk*

When clearing a room, the Marines section it off, with each member assuming responsibility for his portion and shooting any combatants found there. Since surprise and speed play a major role, the room sweeps are fast moving to prevent the enemy from organizing an effective defense. The Marines often toss flash-bang grenades into a room ahead of their entrance to blind, deafen, and confuse any combatants who may be hiding there. *S. F. Tomajczyk*

By helping recruits overcome their fear about being in water over their head and jumping from tall structures, the Combat Water Survival course plays an important role in building confidence.

WEAPONS TRAINING

Since the Marine Corps is the proverbial "tip of the spear" and, as such, is usually the first fighting force to arrive on the scene, every Marine—from private to general—must be a qualified marksman with a rifle. For it is the rifleman who must close with and kill the enemy.

One of the first things a recruit learns when arriving at boot camp is the "My Rifle" creed (see sidebar) which in part states that a Marine must fire true and hit the target he is aiming at, for in battle it is the hit that counts. The Marine also promises to master his rifle, learning its strengths and weaknesses. At some point, rifle and Marine merge and become a deadly weapon. Without each other, they are useless.

From Week 1, when their M16A2 service rifles are issued, recruits spend time every day disassembling, cleaning, and reassembling them. They also receive thorough instruction on the weapon's operation, how to adjust the sight, and how to properly handle and carry it. The training is so detailed that it does not take long before recruits actually begin having dreams about the rifle's eight steps in the cycle of functioning: feeding, chambering, locking, firing, unlocking, extraction, ejection, and cocking.

As for the marksmanship training, it is a progressive, three-phase endeavor. Phase One, Preparatory Marksmanship, teaches recruits the following techniques in sequence:

- Sighting and aiming
- Firing positions (prone, sitting, kneeling, standing)
- Trigger Control
- Rapid Fire
- Sight Adjustments
- Effects of weather on firing and bullet trajectory

Most of these techniques are learned during "Grass Week," which is scheduled for Week 6 at boot camp. Recruits spend their days at the Weapons and Field Training Battalion's firing ranges, each of which is named for an important Marine action during the Korean and Vietnam Wars, such as Inchon, Chosin, and Khe Sanh. They spend hours doing repetitive, and monotonous, "snapping in" drills to learn the proper sequence in loading, aiming, and firing their weapons—without ammunition. But as the instructors promise, if they learn the technique and practice it meticulously, they will become deadly marksmen.

It is during this time that a condition known as "sling paralysis" can occur. It is the impaired function of one or more nerves in the arm, and is caused by a tight rifle sling. The most common signs of sling paralysis are wrist drop, weakness in the backward movement of the arm, and/or numbness over any part of the arm or hand. At the end of each snapping-in period, instructors do a quick test for this ailment by having recruits hold their arms straight forward (palms down), while supporting their rifle by the sling on the back of their hands.

In warfare, the advantage always goes to the force positioned on higher ground. It is easier and more effective to shoot downhill than uphill. Heeding this adage, the Marines attack a building from the top, down. Often times that is achieved by landing on the roof via helicopter, but more often than not it means having to climb up to the highest floor from the ground. Fortunately, a two-story building—which represents the majority of structures on the face of the earth—doesn't present a problem. Marines simply boost a buddy into a window, who then pulls the rest of the team or squad up. Then they go about their deadly work. *S. F. Tomajczyk*

Voice commands in combat are not always wise or possible. For instance, the noise of a battlefield can drown out an order, regardless of how loud it is yelled. Likewise, when conducting a stealthy patrol, noise is not desired, least of all a yelled command. As a result, Marines use arm and hand signals to convey more than 30 specific orders, such as "commence firing," "disperse," and "take cover." In this photo, the leader has given the "halt" command. To be effective, the leader must position himself so the signals can be seen immediately by others. *S. F. Tomajczyk*

During Phase Two, the recruits apply the techniques learned in Phase One to fire at a target at a known distance. This is an extremely important phase because it bridges the theory of snapping in to actually firing live ammunition. By shooting at several distances ranging from 36 yards to 500 yards, the recruit learns firsthand what effect wind and weather have on the bullet. It also reinforces his or her confidence at engaging the enemy at long distances.

At this time, recruits learn just how paranoid "Mother Green"—a nickname for the Corps—is when it comes to accounting for ammunition. Recruits are always given the exact number of rounds needed to complete a firing session. Afterward, they undergo a "shakedown" for any bullets or brass they may have hidden. Pants pockets are turned inside out, and instructors pat them down. Even hand-held metal detectors are sometimes used. Additionally, all magazines and magazine pouches are searched for live or expended ammunition. And just

in case someone manages to somehow slip a bullet off the range and later on feels guilty, brightly painted red "amnesty" boxes are posted in several locations on the ranges. All the person has to do is drop the ammo through a slot, without any fear of punishment.

After four full days of shooting during "Firing Week" (Week 7), recruits qualify with their M16A2 rifles on the last day of known-distance firing. Shooting 50 rounds— each with a maximum score of 5 points for a bulls-eye and 0 for a miss—they must score 190 points or better. (A score of 190 earns a Marksman badge; 210, Sharpshooter; 220, Expert.) Furthermore, they must demonstrate mastery of safe handling and use of the rifle.

The third and last phase is Field Range Firing, in which recruits gain experience in shooting at realistic targets in combatlike surroundings. This involves locating a target using either the hasty search or detailed search method, correctly estimating the range to it, making necessary adjustments to the rifle, and then finally shooting (and hitting) the target. For moving targets, the rifleman must also determine how far ahead of it to aim and fire (a technique known as "leading").

Instructors teach the recruits how to quickly assume any field-firing position, such as shooting from behind a pile of rubble, from a forward slope, from a rooftop, from inside a bunker, from a window, and from a fighting hole (formerly known as a foxhole). They are also taught how to fire their weapon left- and right-handed, how to shoot when wearing a gas mask, and how to provide assault fire when advancing on an enemy position. Many exercises are done during low-light or night conditions, acknowledging the fact that war doesn't end with the setting sun.

While a Marine with a loaded rifle is considered to be a lethal weapon, when a bayonet is affixed to that same rifle, the Marine quickly strikes terror into his enemy. The enemy knows that a skilled and confident Marine can turn the rifle and bayonet into a deadly combination of spear, sword, club, and shield. He knows that the Marine will be ruthless, vicious, and fast in his attack. And he knows that the Marine will never pause until he has won. It is one of the reasons the U.S. Marine Corps is held in such high regard around the world.

THE CRUCIBLE
The last training area that notably influences the metamorphosis of a recruit into a Marine is an event known as the Crucible. Conceived in 1996 by General Charles

A simulated burst of machine-gun fire as these Marine recruits cross a footbridge sends them flying to the dirt. Notice how they fan out slightly to create a defensive position so they can fire back at the enemy. The DIs who accompany the recruits during the Crucible often have them repeat a tactical course (like the one shown here) over and over again. First, it teaches the recruits an important skill that will be used in combat. And second, it tires them physically, mentally and emotionally—because as they near the end of a course and their hopes rise, they are sent back to the start. Fatigue is an ever-present condition during the Crucible. *S. F. Tomajczyk*

The Crucible requires careful planning and logistical coordination. At this facility, Marines track the location and progress of each 18-member team, and orchestrate all operations that occur during the 54-hour event. An aside: if the surrounding scenery looks familiar to you, it should. The movies *The Great Santini*, *The Big Chill*, and *Forrest Gump* were filmed near Parris Island. *S. F. Tomajczyk*

Krulak, 31st Commandant of the Marine Corps, the Crucible is a 54-hour-long event that serves as the culminating event of boot camp and the defining moment in a Marine's new life. It attempts to mimic the rigors and stress of combat by physically, mentally, and emotionally challenging the recruits through strenuous activity, and food and sleep deprivation. The focus of the Crucible is on character development and teamwork among the recruits.

During the 2 1/2-day evolution, the recruits (who are organized in 18-member teams) travel 42 miles on foot while carrying combat gear. They sleep a total of eight hours and eat only 2.5 MREs (Meal, Ready-to-Eat). Along the way, as they become progressively fatigued, they engage in 29 problem-solving exercises and participate in a number of combat-related events, such as unknown-distance firing, combat assault resupply, casualty evacuation, bayonet assault, night infiltration, and hand-to-hand combat.

It all begins in the middle of the night at 0200 hours when they are awoken and sent on a 6-mile forced march to Page Field, an old World War II airfield on Parris Island that serves as the Crucible's playground. From dawn to dusk, the recruits partake in a never-ending series of events.

For instance, in Event 4, the recruits drag water containers, ammunition boxes, and food through the combat assault course, which consists of a tree line, wire fences, trenches, a wall, and an open field. As they carry the heavy supplies through the course, they are greeted with simulated weapons fire, including machine guns and artillery. The explosions, which are caused by high-pressure gas, are extremely realistic—the overpressure thumps the chest and the sharp blast leaves the ears ringing.

In a psychological twist, loudspeakers broadcast blood-chilling screams and the mournful cries of soldiers whimpering, "Momma! Momma! Oh god, Momma!" If you close your eyes, you can easily envision yourself on a

Making sound decisions when tired and stressed is vitally important on the battlefield. To simulate that, the Crucible includes a number of leadership reaction courses, each of which tests the recruits' ability to work as a team to solve problems. In this photo, a recruit begins one course problem by crawling through a pipe. Using three wooden boards, he and his team members will have to cross a number of stumps located at the other end of the pipe without touching the ground. *S. F. Tomajczyk*

battlefield. In fact, you involuntarily duck when a simulated grenade explodes nearby.

This resupply exercise is immediately followed by four Warrior stations—each named for an enlisted Marine who received the Medal of Honor. When the recruits arrive at a station, one of them reads aloud how the hero's actions exemplify the Corps and its values.

The four Warrior stations associated with Event 4 are:

- **Corporal John Mackie's Passage**—Team members must pass horizontally through a truck tire that is suspended by four cables without touching the tire.
- **Sergeant Gonzalez's Crossing**—Teams cross over a contaminated area by swinging on ropes from one "safe spot" to another.
- **Private First Class Anderson's Fall**—Team members fall backward from a raised platform into the arms of their comrades.
- **Private Cecula's Wall**—Teams climb a 10-foot wall and climb down the other side using a knotted rope.

When these assignments are finished, the recruits move on to Event 5, a confidence course with four different problem-solving exercises, and Event 6, unknown-distance firing from simulated building structures and a 250-meter casualty evacuation. After a quick MRE for dinner, they are herded back into the palmetto groves and scrub pines to conduct a night-infiltration exercise. That is immediately followed by a 5-mile forced march, which ends around midnight. Only then are the recruits finally permitted to curl up inside their tents at the bivouac site and get some sleep.

Four hours later, they are awoken. The second day of the Crucible has begun.

As this routine suggests, the Crucible is intense. It is, after all, where Marines are forged. Recruits quickly realize that the only way they will survive is by coming together as a unit. There is strength in unity. They must win as one, or fail miserably. Together, they are stronger than the pain that throbs inside them.

With each step taken and every obstacle successfully overcome, the recruits' determination grows. When one falls, the others pick him up.

Can't is not in their vocabulary.

Failure is not an option.

They learn to improvise, adapt, and overcome. The only thing they focus on is success. None want to give up.

Appropriately, the Crucible ends with the rising sun. Reveille is at 0300 hours and, an hour later, the recruits begin a 9-mile forced march to the finish line. Their legs hurt. They stink to high heaven. Their clothing is soiled black. They have blisters on their hands and feet. And many are hallucinating from the lack of sleep, while others stare blankly ahead.

At first, the recruits stumble along in the darkness, the rank and file expanding and contracting like a

Recruits learn basic rappelling and fast-roping techniques on this six-story-high tower. The metal skid seen at the top left of the tower is from an UH-1 Iroquois (a.k.a. Huey) helicopter, a variant of which is still in service with the Marine Corps as a command-and-control aircraft. It is also used for special operations missions. *S. F. Tomajczyk*

AN OFFICER AND A GENTLEMAN

If a Marine is a member of the few and the proud, a Marine officer arguably belongs to the fewer and prouder. In an armed service with only 174,000 Marines, officers represent less than 10 percent. The Marine Corps has the highest enlisted-to-officer ratio among all America's military forces.

Since an officer is a leader of Marines, the Corps seeks only the best individuals to lead by example while under demanding conditions. This is an extremely important trait; the Marine Corps does everything it can to ensure that candidates are mentally and physically prepared for the task.

Unlike other military services, the Marine Corps does not have its own academy as its primary source of officers, although the U.S. Naval Academy permits up to 16 percent of graduating midshipmen to become Marines. Hence, the road to a commission as a Second Lieutenant begins with one of several programs at Officer Candidates School (OCS): Naval Reserve Officer Training Corps, Platoon Leaders Class, and Officer Candidate Class. There is even a program to encourage enlisted Marines to "mustang" and cross over the line to officer territory—the Enlisted Commissioning Program.

Regardless of which path is taken, the Officer Candidates School trains, evaluates, and carefully screens applicants to make certain they have the mettle and leadership abilities ultimately to be an officer of Marines. (About 25 percent do not.) The motto of OCS is *"Ductus Exemplo"* (Leadership by Example), and the staff expects no less from the candidates. Placing them under extreme and prolonged stress during the 10-week course, the staff constantly monitors the candidates to see if indeed they are able to manage time wisely, inspire and lead their peers, and successfully accomplish all assigned missions and tasks.

Passing OCS means being deemed qualified to be trained. After being commissioned in the Marine Corps as second lieutenants, the newly minted "butter bars" are sent to Quantico, Virginia, to attend the Basic School (TBS) – the officer's equivalent of boot camp. There, they are indoctrinated in the duties of infantry leaders. This is important because regardless of which military specialty a Marine officer pursues, he is expected to be able to successfully serve as a platoon commander and lead Marines into battle.

Over the course of six months at TBS, the officers learn the intricacies of a wide range of military topics, including:

- Land navigation
- Communications
- Combat intelligence
- Military law
- Amphibious operations
- Nuclear, biological, and chemical warfare defense
- Combat tactics (e.g., patrolling, urban warfare, night attack)
- Fire support coordination
- Weapons
- Close-air support and helicopter operations
- Field engineering
- Terrorism and counterinsurgency

The culminating event at the Basic School is "War Week," five continuous days of simulated combat, in which the lieutenants learn what it is like to lead a platoon on the battlefield. The various scenarios and missions they are exposed to in the field on a 24-hour basis allow them to exercise all they have been taught, such as calling for close-air support, responding to a chemical attack, and conducting maneuver warfare. They also learn how to bear physical exhaustion, lack of food, and sleep deprivation. Overall, the experience teaches them how to be flexible and creative, while controlling panic and clearing the "fog of war" from their heads so they can make sound tactical decisions.

OCS candidates conduct a 2-mile-long ammunition resupply mission
over rugged terrain at The Basic School.

Throughout their stay at TBS, the performance of all officer students is closely evaluated by the training staff. Those who do not measure up to the standards are dropped from the school, their commissions are revoked, and they return to civilian life.

For those Marine officers who endure the rigorous training, they graduate from the Basic School possessing the confidence, skills, and demeanor to command Marines. They also possess "high-speed, chaos-proof leadership." That ability in itself often means the difference between success and failure, and—in combat—life and death.

drunken caterpillar moving along a tree limb. When the horizon finally lightens and the sound of birds fills the air, their hearts soar. The end is at hand. They've made it. They have been torn down and completely rebuilt. In a week, they will finally receive the Globe-and-Anchor emblem and, with it, the coveted title of U.S. Marine.

Their pace picks up and they march with pride, Jody calls echoing in the morning mist. Ahead is the Warriors' Breakfast back at the battalion—all you can eat steak, eggs, and potatoes.

EMBLEM CEREMONY

The week after completing the Crucible is known as "Transition Week." The days are used by the recruits to recover from their ordeal and to begin transitioning from boot camp to membership in the Marine Corps. As part of that process, the drill instructors back off on their discipline. That must now come from each recruit himself.

But the DIs continue to mentor the recruits, reinforcing traditional customs and courtesies, core values, and *esprit de corps*.

With boot camp coming to an end, the recruits reflect on just how far they have come. In the past 12 weeks they have each fired 633 rounds with the M16 service rifle, hiked 64 miles, and run 61.5 miles. Additionally, they have passed the Combat Water Survival test, passed the physical fitness test, and scored a minimum of 80 percent on a series of written and practical exams that test mastery of Marine Corps common skills. Further, each has become certified as a tan belt in the Marine Corps Martial Arts Program, rappelled down a 40-foot tower, been exposed to a chemical warfare agent, passed the Recruit Training Battalion Commander's inspection, and completed the Crucible. It has been a tremendous journey, one that literally started with a step—the yellow footsteps painted on the pavement in front of the Receiving Barracks.

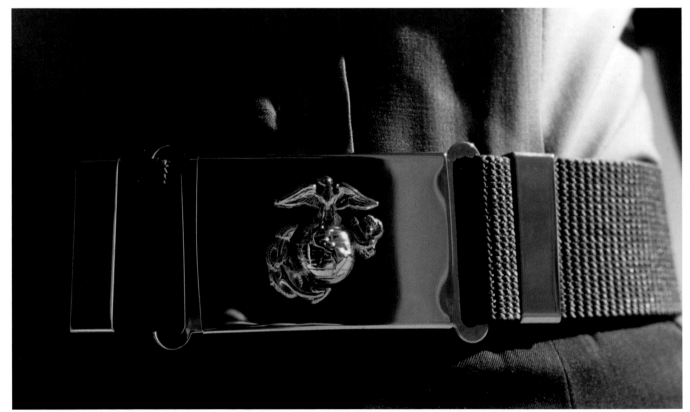

This beautifully polished belt buckle with the Marine emblem is part of the brightwork, a term that refers to any metallic item in the uniform. It is probably the brightest and most prominent item on this Marine recruit's uniform. Civilians often wonder why Marines don't wear shoulder patches, cords, decals, loops, and other such devices. As far as the Marine Corps is concerned, those items are not needed. The Globe and Anchor is all that is needed to identify them. Anything else on the Marine uniform is *earned*. S. F. Tomajczyk

A platoon of Marines has just received and pinned the Marine Corps emblem on their hats, also known as cover. It's a proud and emotional moment for them as they face the stands where their families are now standing, shouting, and applauding their accomplishment. *S. F. Tomajczyk*

A color guard heralds the much-awaited Emblem Ceremony, which is held the day before graduation. Recruits actually look forward to this moment more than graduation for three reasons: (1) They earn the title of Marine; (2) They get to see their family for the first time in three months; and (3) They get the rest of the day off for liberty. *S. F. Tomajczyk*

A week after completing the Crucible, a platoon of Marines with their senior drill instructor stand proud just minutes after receiving their Globe and Anchor. As the Marine Corps' recruiting materials state: "Once a Man has walked through fire and survived, little else can burn." That's a perfect description of boot camp. *S. F. Tomajczyk*

Left: The battalion commander's inspection is the last inspection the recruits undergo before graduating from boot camp. For many recruits it is also the most intimidating and nerve-wracking experience of their 12-week-long ordeal. As the commander (usually a lieutenant colonel) rakes over your uniform with hawklike eyes, he—or in this photo, she—asks monotone questions like, "Who is the assistant secretary of defense?" or "What is the seventh General Order?" The recruit is graded on everything, including his or her answers. Although Marines eat a lot of food during basic training—upward of 4,300 calories a day—by this point they have actually lost so much weight that their uniforms need tailoring. In fact, it is the most common observation a battalion commander makes during the inspection. *S. F. Tomajczyk*

Below: A miniature of the Iwo Jima Memorial sits adjacent to the Peatross Parade Deck, serving as a constant reminder of the dedication and sacrifice the Marine Corps makes to America. In the past, recruits who completed the Crucible were marched directly to the statue, where they were given their "Globe and Anchor" emblem and officially recognized as Marines. Today, however, they must wait a week. The change was made to keep the traditions between San Diego (which does not have an Iwo Jima memorial) and Parris Island the same. *S. F. Tomajczyk*

A Marine receives hugs from family members. The U.S. Marine Corps has a special ethos, a special culture. Ask any Marine what he does and he or she will reply, "I'm a Marine." With the other armed services, the answer is "I'm a pilot" or "I'm a Ranger." But for Marines, they are always a Marine first. *S. F. Tomajczyk*

On Training Day 69 (TD-69), the recruits find themselves standing proudly at attention on the enormous Peatross Parade Deck, their families and friends cheering in the bleachers. It is time for the Marine Corps Emblem Ceremony. On their uniform they wear the insignia of rank for the first time: Private (E-1) or Private First Class (E-2), depending on their enlistment contract. In a few instances, some are meritoriously promoted to Lance Corporal (E-3) for having demonstrated outstanding leadership potential.

Over the loudspeaker, the battalion commander congratulates the recruits on their accomplishment and then orders them to pin the Eagle, Globe, and Anchor emblem on their hats. While the Drill Instructors pass out the emblems, Lee Greenwood's "Proud To Be An American" resonates through the air—bringing tears to everyone's eyes.

They are no longer recruits. In fact, that term will never be used in any form in reference to them again. They are Marines.

Tomorrow may officially be graduation, but they became Marines today. In the words of the battalion commander:

"You have come a long way . . . I am extremely proud of each of you and salute all of you for everything you have achieved here in your training. As you prepare to depart Parris Island, allow me to offer you this simple advice. Always remember who you are, what you are, and, most importantly, what you have the potential to become. I wish each of you good luck, Godspeed, and *Semper Fidelis*.

"Ladies and gentlemen, I present to you the newest Marines of our Corps."

THREE

An aerial view of the USS *Bataan* (LHD-5). The largest amphibious assault ships in the world, these *Wasp*-class ships accommodate 1,894 Marines as well as 30 helicopters and 6 to 10 AV-8B Harrier jump jets. In their stern deck, they hold 3 air-cushioned landing craft (LCAC). They are capable of projecting tremendous military power anywhere in the world. *S. F. Tomajczyk*

Soldiers of the Sea

The deadliest weapon in the world is a Marine and his rifle.
General John J. Pershing, U.S. Army

*The Marine Corps is proud of the fact that it is a force of combined arms,
and it jealously guards the integrity of its air-ground team.*
General Keith B. McCutcheon, USMC
Naval Review, 1971

During times of peace, the most important task of any military is to prepare for war. That's because if other nations perceive that another country's military force is capable of immediately and violently waging war, it can actually serve as a deterrent and thereby thwart aggression. As the United States' force-in-readiness, the Marine Corps continually maintains itself for immediate employment in any clime and place, and in any type of conflict. As a result, all its peacetime activities are focused on achieving combat readiness.

Before newly minted enlisted Marines are permitted to join ground combat units from boot camp, they must first graduate from the School of Infantry, where they are taught (among many things) small unit tactics, demolition, and heavy weapons. The Marine Corps has two of these schools: one at Camp Lejeune, North Carolina, and the other at Camp Pendleton, California.

While boot camp training does indeed provide Marines with a common experience, a proud heritage, a set of values, and a common bond of comradeship, it is still only the first step in the forging of a Marine warrior. It does not, for instance, provide the combat skills and the unit formations and attack tactics required to actually fight in a battle.

That task is reserved for the School of Infantry. One way to look at this is that if boot camp makes "basic Marines," the School of Infantry makes "monster Marines."

The School of Infantry has two different training programs, the Infantry Training Battalion and the Marine Combat Training Battalion.

A CH-53 Super Stallion conducts a vertical replenishment (VERTREP) operation aboard the flight deck of the USS *Bataan*. The helicopter is strong enough to lift 16 tons of cargo slung beneath it. Based on this, the Super Stallion can lift 90 percent of the combat equipment used by a Marine division. *S. F. Tomajczyk*

INFANTRY TRAINING BATTALION

This 52-day program is for future "grunts," Marines who serve in military occupational specialties (MOS) as infantrymen, machine gunners, mortar men, assault men, and antitank guided missile men.

The infantrymen (MOS 0311) conduct most of their training out in the field, where they concentrate on patrolling, offensive and defensive operations, and military operations in urban terrain.

The machine gunners (MOS 0331) learn how to effectively employ heavy automatic weapons like the M240G 7.62mm medium machine gun, the M2 .50-caliber heavy machine gun, and the Mk. 19 40mm automatic grenade launcher, which fires a variety of grenades out to a maximum range of 2,200 meters.

The mortar men (MOS 0341) learn how to fire the M224 60mm lightweight mortar and the M252 81mm medium extended-range mortar, and use them to support combat operations.

The so-called "assault men" (MOS 0351) are rocket and demolitions specialists who are trained to use the Mk. 153 shoulder-launched, multipurpose assault weapon (SMAW) and the Javelin fire-and-forget antitank missile. They are also skilled in using explosives.

And last, the antitank guided missile men (MOS 0352) are taught how to attack enemy tanks and armored

MARINE CORPS WAY OF LIFE

Unlike other military services, which often unwind after hours and on weekends, being a Marine is truly a way of life. The Corps thoroughly permeates and influences a Marine's actions on a 24/7 basis. Here are a few words of wisdom that Marines heed:

- Conduct yourself with dignity, courtesy, and self-restraint.
- Never speak ill of the Corps in the presence of civilians or members of the other armed forces.
- Avoid any show of self-importance.
- Do not make the same mistake twice.
- Be punctual; always be five minutes early.
- Do not complain, and avoid those who do.
- Be industrious, attentive to duty, and persevering.
- Control and hide your feelings.
- Always be alert and look alert.
- Do not procrastinate, and do more than you are told to do.
- Stand straight, and keep your hands out of your pockets.
- Never chew gum or smoke in public.
- Do not carry packages when in uniform.
- Never appear unshaven after 8:00 a.m.
- Stay fit.
- Go through proper channels. Do not go over people's heads or infringe on someone's area of responsibility.
- Keep your uniforms in pristine shape, brightware spotlessly clean, and ensure that ribbons and insignias are in their proper positions.
- Do not wear jewelry, or pens or pencils exposed on the uniform, except for wrist watch, regulation tie-clasp, and rings.
- Maintain a neat and close-trimmed haircut.

vehicles using several different weapon systems, including the tube-launched, optically tracked, wire-guided (TOW) missile.

All of these specialists go through the same identical training during the first 14 training days. Referred to as the "Common Skills Package," the curriculum addresses basic combat skills such as target engagement, hand grenades, M249 light machine gun employment, offensive tactics, mines, AT-4 shoulder-fired antiarmor rocket, fire and movement methods, NBC protection and decontamination, land navigation, patrolling techniques, and urban warfare. Then, on the 15th day the Marines break off and begin learning their specialties.

MARINE COMBAT TRAINING BATTALION

Not all Marines serve in the infantry. There are those who work in intelligence, communications, electronic warfare, vehicle repair, public affairs, nuclear and biochemical defense, logistics, and more. These individuals—and all female enlisted Marines—attend 14 training days at the Marine Combat Training Battalion to learn the infantry skills essential to operate in a combat environment.

That's because while they may not actually be located in battlefield trenches, they could easily find themselves serving in a rear-echelon area that could come under enemy attack. In those instances, they need to know how to use grenades and machine guns, as well as how to employ effective combat formations. Even in the absence of an attack, they must know how to conduct security patrols, camouflage gear, and set up defenses.

Upon completion of the School of Infantry, most of the Marines are finally integrated into Marine Corps units. The remainder, who are generally specializing in more complex military operations, go on to receive advanced training in such areas as aviation, artillery, engineering, intelligence, and communications.

Later on, as the Marines are promoted up through the ranks and acquire more experience, they could find themselves qualifying to undergo training to become a Scout-Sniper or Drill Instructor, or even to join the elite Force Recon or Marine Security Guard battalions. Regardless of the training opportunities, Marines must keep in mind that in spite of their military specialty, they must always be prepared for all appropriate duties of their rank. They are first and foremost, Marines. They are riflemen. They are defenders of the United States of America.

Left: A glance inside the hectic world of PriFly aboard the USS *Nassau* (LHA-4). The air boss (right) and mini boss (left) coordinate the launch and recovery of all aircraft on the flight deck. As with an aircraft carrier, they own all the airspace out to 10 miles from the ship. When a helicopter or Harrier lands aboard an amphibious assault ship, it flies up the starboard side of the ship, crosses the bow, and then approaches the designated landing spot (one of nine) from the port side. This simple procedure becomes more hazardous during stormy weather and during night operations, when pilots wear night-vision goggles. *S. F. Tomajczyk*

Right: Unlike an aircraft carrier, an amphibious assault ship does not use a catapult to launch its helicopters and Harriers. This causes a dilemma since every aircraft model has different aerodynamics. Complicating matters is the fact that air does not flow uniformly over the amphibious assault ship's flight deck; swirls and eddies routinely form. What this means is that the air boss and mini boss must calculate the "wind envelope" for each aircraft before a launch or recovery attempt is made. They use a device called a "whiz" to determine what direction the ship should be turned in—taking into consideration the wind and other environmental factors—to facilitate a safe launch or landing. They provide the directions to the ship's bridge by phone. *S. F. Tomajczyk*

The USS *Whidbey Island* (LSD-41) returns to Little Creek, Virginia, at dawn after finishing an at-sca training exercise. Internally, she has 12,500 square feet of storage space for tanks and combat vehicles, plus 5,000 cubic feet of space for cargo and provisions. Her rear well deck accommodates four LCACs or 64 amphibious assault vehicles. *S. F. Tomajczyk*

The fast-combat support ship the USS *Seattle* (AOE-3) conducts an underway replenishment (UNREP) of the USS *Bataan* at dusk. For nearly an hour, cargo, fuel, and provisions are sent across by cable. During this entire time, the two ships must synchronize their speed and heading. *S. F. Tomajczyk*

THE DOGS OF WAR

In June 1918, the Marines of the 4th Brigade joined up with the Army's 2nd Division to dislodge German soldiers entrenched on the strategic heights of Belleau Wood, a 20-acre plateau. The battle raged for three weeks, and the Marines fought so ferociously that the Germans reported to headquarters they had encountered highly trained shock troops—referring to them as *teufelhunden* (devil dogs), the violent mountain dogs of Bavarian folklore.

Even though Molly is a Marine mascot, she doesn't catch any slack from the drill instructor, who ensures her boot camp is as demanding as any Marine recruit's.

Soon thereafter, a Marine Corps' recruiting poster appeared that depicted a snarling bulldog wearing a USMC helmet. The image was so beloved by the public and Marines alike, that the resolute and malevolent English Bulldog has been the Corps' unofficial mascot ever since.

The first bulldog to be enlisted was Jiggs. In 1922, Brigadier General Smedley D. Butler signed an official waiver allowing Private Jiggs to avoid boot camp and to serve in the Marine Corps for life. He sported a custom-made uniform as he went about his inspirational duties in the Corps. As a result of his dedication and hard work, Jiggs was quickly promoted to corporal (E-4) and then sergeant (E-5) and, in 1924, all the way to sergeant major (E-9). His untimely death in 1927 was mourned throughout the Marine Corps. As a special honor, Sgt. Maj. Jiggs lay in state at Quantico Marine Corps Base, and he was finally interred with full military honors.

Today, mascots continue to serve with a number of individual Marine Corps units, including the Marine Corps Recruit Depot San Diego (Molly), Marine Corps Recruit Depot Parris Island (Mac), Marine Corps Recruiting Substation Plano, Texas (Stinky), Marine Corps Base Hawaii (Danno), II Marine Expeditionary Force (Chopper IV), and Marine Barracks 8th and I, Washington, D.C. (Chesty).

SEND IN THE MARINES!
THE MARINE AIR-GROUND TASK FORCE (MAGTF) AND ITS COMPONENTS

Since World War II, the call "Send in the Marines!" has been sounded more than 200 times—an average of once every 90 days. This demonstrates the confidence the President and other national leaders have in the Marine Corps to successfully carry out a mission. Within the military establishment, many joke that the Marine Corps is America's weapon of mass destruction— "When it absolutely, positively must be destroyed overnight." As is inherent in all jests, there is truth to this one, for the destructive power unleashed by the Marine Corps rests in the unique way the Corps is organized.

This is important to note because the Marine Corps by and large uses the same weapons as the other services, such as the M16 service rifle, 155mm howitzer, F/A-18 Hornet fighter, C-130 Hercules transport, and the M1A1 Abrams tank. So it is what the Marines do with these tools and the way they employ their use on the battlefield that makes the difference. They do not have a hidden stash of proton-beam weapons, reverberating carbonizer handguns, or Star Wars-like light sabers (although enemy soldiers may insist otherwise, and some Marines may give a knowing, smug grin).

The major operational branch of the Marines is the Marine Corps Operating Forces, the principal combat arm of which is the Fleet Marine Forces (FMF). At any given time, about 65 percent of the Marine Corps—some 112,000 Marines—are assigned to separate FMFs in the Pacific and Atlantic areas, where they are under the orders of the Navy operating forces, and are constantly preparing to be deployed. (FMF Atlantic is a component of the unified U.S. Atlantic Command; FMF Pacific, U.S. Pacific Command.) Each FMF is a combined-arms force composed of a headquarters unit, three combat divisions, three aircraft wings, and three service support groups.

Unlike the Navy, Army, Air Force, and Coast Guard, the Marines rely on an integrated "package" of air power, combat forces, field support units, and command and control elements to wage war. From historical experience, they have learned that coordination among these four areas is critical to the success of military operations. Collectively, these components make up what is known as a Marine Air-Ground Task Force (MAGTF).

These old, beat-up looking jeeps are still in use by the Marines because they fit perfectly inside a CH-53 Super Stallion helicopter. That enables the Marines to literally drive out the rear ramp and into the heat of battle. This concept embraces the adage, "Improvise, Adapt, and Overcome!" *S. F. Tomajczyk*

Two "Humvees" race over the sand during a training exercise at Onslow Beach at Camp Lejeune in North Carolina. These mobile, four-wheel-drive tactical vehicles have been configured for many purposes since their introduction in the U.S. military, including ambulance, cargo/troop carrier, TOW antitank missile carrier, and armament carrier. *S. F. Tomajczyk*

The MAGTF (pronounced "mag-taff") is organized, trained, and equipped to respond to crises and conduct warfare across three dimensions: air, land, and sea. It provides commanders with versatile and scalable forces that are capable of responding to a broad range of incidents, such as providing disaster relief, evacuating embassies, or conducting combat operations.

Although there are four different sizes of MAGTF—each projecting different levels of force—*every* MAGTF has the following four elements:

Command Element

All battles need someone to orchestrate the movement of infantrymen, aircraft, and other combat forces so they can be effectively used against the enemy. The command element provides this direction and control, as well as surveillance, reconnaissance, intelligence, and communications efforts.

Ground Combat Element

These are the so-called "ground pounders" who actually do the fighting. The element is a unit made up of infantry, tanks, and assault vehicles that are reinforced with the necessary artillery, antitank, transport, combat engineer, and reconnaissance assets to accomplish the mission at hand.

Aviation Combat Element

These individuals provide air power and aerial support to the MAGTF. The unit is composed of air-control agencies, helicopter and fixed-wing squadrons, surface-to-air missile units, aerial reconnaissance and electronic warfare capabilities (including active and passive electronic countermeasures), and aviation-specific combat service support. As a collateral function, the assigned Marine aircraft wing may also provide units that operate alongside Navy assets aboard aircraft carriers.

A view from "vulture's row" on the USS *John F. Kennedy* (CV-67) shows an F-14 Tomcat (front) and an F/A-18 Hornet (rear) preparing to launch off the aircraft carrier's waist catapults. Most people do not realize that the Marine Corps flies fighters in support of amphibious and combat operations. In this photo, the F/A-18 is actually a Marine jet assigned to VFMA-251. The Hornet was America's first strike fighter, and it is now the backbone of naval aviation. Its missions include air superiority, precision strike, and ground attack. *S. F. Tomajczyk*

A quiet end to a busy day aboard the USS *Bataan*. Three Marines chat among themselves at the ship's stern in the shadow of the AV-8B Harrier, a single-engine, vertical/short takeoff and landing (V/STOL) aircraft used by the Marine Corps for light attack and close-air support roles. It has a combat range of 165 miles carrying 12 500-pound bombs, with one-hour loiter. A wide variety of pods, dispensers, fuel tanks, and weapons can be slung from the six wing pylons, including B-61 nuclear bombs. The aircraft is also armed with a five-barrel 25mm cannon with 300 rounds. *S. F. Tomajczyk*

Combat Service Support Element

A military force cannot operate on empty stomachs, empty weapons, or empty gas tanks. This element provides the full range of services necessary to sustain and maintain the MAGTF, such as medical and dental care, food supplies, ammunition, fuel, data processing, military police, and vehicle maintenance units. Through its efforts, the CSSE enables a MAGTF to operate in austere combat environments for extended periods of time.

THE MARINE EXPEDITIONARY FORCE (MEF)

The largest MAGTF is the Marine expeditionary force (MEF), and unlike other MAGTFs, it exists both in times of peace and war. (All other MAGTFs are task-organized for specific missions and, after completion of those missions, are dissolved.) The MEF is the Marine Corps' large,

butt-kicking, war-fighting organization and, as such, is made up of 20,000 to 90,000 Marines and sailors, as well as 233 amphibious assault vehicles, 130 light armored vehicles, 58 M1A1 tanks, 72 155mm howitzers, 84 F/A-18 fighters, 182 helicopters, 60 AV-8B Harrier jets, and 161 short- and long-range mortars.

The Marine Corps maintains three standing Marine expeditionary forces, each commanded by a lieutenant general and each strategically positioned for global coverage. I MEF, based in California and Arizona, and III MEF, which is forward-based in Okinawa, mainland Japan, and Hawaii, fall under the control of the commander of Marine Forces, Pacific (MARFORPAC). II MEF, which is located at bases in North Carolina and South Carolina, falls under the control of the commander of Marine Forces, Atlantic (MARFORLANT). All three MEFs are intentionally located near major naval bases, airports, railroads, highways, and seaports, ensuring the rapid deployment of Marine combat power worldwide.

Equipped with 60 days of supplies, the powerful MEFs are capable of both amphibious operations and sustained combat operations ashore in virtually any geographic location, either independently or as part of a joint warfighting effort. Depending on the mission requirements, an MEF can be customized to accentuate a particular capability. For instance, when conducting operations in jungles or cities, the MEF may deploy without its heavier mechanized units, such as the M1A1 tanks. On the other hand, for high-intensity operations, it may be reinforced with armored, artillery, and air units. The unique power of the MEF is that it can be instantly tailored to meet the needs of the situation at hand.

The MEF serves as the reservoir from which the following, smaller MAGTFs originate.

MARINE EXPEDITIONARY BRIGADE (MEB)

This is a midsized MAGTF that is made up of 3,000 to 20,000 Marines, under the command of a brigadier general. Each of the three MEFs has a Marine expeditionary brigade within its structure, with the deputy MEF commander serving as the MEB commander. The air-ground task force essentially responds to small-scale contingencies, or it serves as a transitional military force that assists a Marine expeditionary unit (MEU)—usually the first on the scene of a crisis—until the entire MEF arrives, if necessary. An MEB, which is equipped with enough supplies for 30 days, is capable of rapid deployment via amphibious ships (usually 15, including 5 large-deck assault ships) or strategic airlift.

The most highly specialized MEB in the Marine Corps is the 4th Marine Expeditionary Brigade (Antiterrorism), which was established in the aftermath of the September 11, 2001, terrorist attacks. The 4th MEB(AT) is assigned to

The flight deck of the USS *Bataan* is crowded with aircraft that are ready to wage war. In the foreground is the AH-1W Super Cobra attack helicopter, a deadly aircraft that provides air support to the assault force. The flight deck can accommodate 24 helicopters and six Harriers. The CH-46 Sea Knights are usually parked toward the bow ("forward bone") while the CH-53 Super Stallions and AV-8B Harriers are spotted to the stern ("rear bone"). In some situations, such as bad weather, all aircraft are parked in the below-deck hangar in an exercise known as StuffEx (or max pack). It takes about six hours to accomplish this task, with the aircraft crammed in like sardines—with just inches to spare between them. *S. F. Tomajczyk*

FAVORITE MARINE CORPS BUMPER STICKERS

Deadliest Weapon in the World:
A Marine and His Rifle

Marines Never Die…
They Just Go to Hell and Re-Group

Marines Always Welcome
Relatives by Appointment

On the Eighth Day
God Created Marines

USMC
Uncle Sam's Misguided Children

Forget Smith and Wesson
This Property Protected by a U.S. Marine

To Err is Human, To Forgive is Divine
However, Neither is Marine Corps Policy

USMC
When It Absolutely, Positively
Must be Destroyed Overnight!

There are Two Types of People:
Marines And Those Who Wish They Were

Be Safe
Sleep with a Marine

Heaven Won't Take Us
And Hell's Afraid We'll Take Over

Mess with One Marine
You Mess with Them ALL

The Impossible Is Done with The Lord's Help
And a Few Good Men

Women Marines
Fewer, Prouder

All Men Are Created Equal,
Then Some Became Marines

No Promises, No Shortcuts
No Retreat, No Surrender

Marines Pull Duty in Heaven
Who Else Would God Trust?

If Everyone Could Get In,
It Wouldn't Be the Marines

You Can Take the Marine Out of the Corps,
But You Can't Take the Corps Out of the Marine

USMC Artillery
A Grunt's Favorite Music

Marine: Your Best Friend
Your Worst Enemy

It's God's Job to Forgive Bin Laden
It's Our Job to Arrange the Meeting

It's Not an Attitude Problem,
We ARE That Good!

The Marines Are Not a Branch
We Are a Breed

Death Smiles at Everyone
Marines Smile Back

To Boldly Go Where a Few Good Men
Have Gone Before

It Ain't Bragging if YOU Can Do It

USMC Is Part of the Navy
The Men's Department

Pain Is Only Temporary
Pride Is Forever

The Marine Corps Doesn't Build Character
It Reveals It

When the Experts Panic
They Call the Marines

FMF Atlantic and is tasked with deterring, detecting, and defending against terrorist threats worldwide, as well as conducting an initial response to chemical and biological incidents. It is made up of four special units.

CHEMICAL, BIOLOGICAL INCIDENT RESPONSE FORCE (CBIRF)

This is a 380-member team established in April 1996 and currently based at Indian Head, Maryland. Its mission is to improve America's ability to rapidly respond to chemical and biological terrorist attacks, such as the one involving the Tokyo subway system. CBIRF personnel respond to

incidents at Navy and State Department facilities around the world. They identify threats, secure and decontaminate areas, treat casualties, and bolster local hospitals' treatment capabilities. The team is equipped to detect and identify 120,000 toxic industrial chemicals, all known chemical warfare agents, eight biological agents, and radiological emissions. A 90-member Initial Response Force maintains a 24-hour readiness posture in the event of a terrorist incident. It can deploy via ground transportation within one hour of notification, or by designated airport within four hours of notification. When required, CBIRF has a follow-on force of 200 specialists to provide ongoing

Left: Heavily armed and wearing a gas mask to avoid being affected by any tear gas that may be used, Marines of the 31st MEU/SOC practice searching a seized ship. One of the first things they do is take over the bridge and engine room so they are in control of the ship. *U.S. Navy*

A candidate at the Marine Security Guard school at Quantico, Virginia, who has been doused with tear gas, learns to control his panic and pain so that he can continue focusing on the task at hand. In this case, it's handling an unruly and aggressive individual (punching bag) with a reverse spin with his baton.

operations. Civilian authorities can even request assistance from the CBIRF for incidents occurring at Olympic events, national political arenas, or other venues. For instance, the team was deployed in the fall of 2001 to handle the anthrax situation in Washington, D.C.

SECURITY FORCE BATTALION

This battalion provides armed antiterrorism personnel to naval installations and units that would be of great interest to terrorists and maintains a worldwide presence at 14 different locations, ranging from Keflavik, Iceland, to Guantanamo Bay, Cuba. These Marines protect key assets, including strategic weapons, command-and-control facilities, and intelligence-gathering sites. Aboard ships, such as aircraft carriers, they safeguard classified information and protect sensitive areas of the vessel. The battalion maintains two fleet antiterrorism security team (FAST) companies—each composed of three 52-man platoons—for immediate deployment worldwide. These Marines receive special training in counterterrorist operations, hostage rescue, and close-quarters combat. They protect facilities against terrorist attack and sabotage. In recent years, FAST responded to the embassy bombings in Dar es Salaam, Tanzania, and Kenya (1998), offered support to the USS *Cole* in Yemen (2000), provided security for the hospital ship USNS *Comfort* in New York City Harbor following the terrorist attack on the World Trade Center (2001), and participated in Operation Iraqi Freedom (2003).

SECURITY GUARD BATTALION

Security guards for select American embassies, consulates, and legations are from this battalion. The Marine Corps presently maintains more than 140 U.S. State Department security detachments, varying in size from 6 to 36 Marines, in most of the capital cities of the world. Each detachment is independently commanded by a staff NCO, the only situation in the Corps in which a noncommissioned officer has his own command. Within each diplomatic mission, the Marine guard is under the operational command of the embassy security officer and the ambassador. Contrary to popular belief, Marine security guards do not defend the entire compound. The detachment's responsibility is mainly defensive in nature: to safeguard classified material and protect embassy staff and property. Security outside the embassy is the responsibility of the host nation.

ANTITERRORISM BATTALION (ATBN)

The antiterrorism battalion is specially trained and equipped to attack terrorists and subversive organizations. While a normal Marine infantry battalion is required to do many tasks, the ATBN focuses solely on detection, deterrence, and defense against terrorism worldwide. As a result, every Marine in the battalion maintains very high marksmanship skills. This is achieved through the Enhanced Marksmanship Program (EMP) course. The EMP is a core skill for the battalion and requires a significant amount of ammunition to maintain. (The ATBN's 5.56 ammunition allocation is five times that of a normal infantry battalion for any fiscal year—1.5 million rounds as opposed to 300,000 for an infantry battalion.) The marksmanship skills apply to pistol and shotgun applications as well. The ATBN routinely has access to

BROTHER MARINES

Although the U.S. Marine Corps is the world's largest, it is certainly not the oldest. Ever since ships have sailed on the high seas, they have needed armed marines to fend off attackers. Here is a partial listing of distinguished "brother marines" from around the world and the year in which they were established.

- Spanish Marines (Intanteria de la Marina Espanola)—1571
- The Royal Marines—1664
- Royal Netherlands Marines (Korps Mariners)—1665
- Brazilian Marine Corps (Corpo do Fusileiros Navais)—1808 (although their lineage to the Portuguese Marines goes back to 1797)
- Argentine Marine Corps—1807
- Colombian Marine Corps—1811
- Venezuelan Marine Corps—1822
- Marine Corps of the Republic of China (Taiwan)—1917
- Royal Thai Marine Corps—1932
- Republic of Korea Marine Corps—1949

Source: The Marine Officer's Guide

An LAV-25 configured as a command-and-control vehicle offloads from the experimental high-speed vessel *Joint Venture* (HSV-X1) at Camp Pendleton, California. The ship is a high-speed (40-plus knots) catamaran that can operate in the shallow waters of the world to land Marine fighting forces. The *Joint Venture* successfully participated in Operation Iraqi Freedom in 2003. *U.S. Navy*

weapons and technologies that normal Marine infantry battalions do not have, such as advanced rifles, advanced optics, and night vision capability, advanced communications, advanced bulletproof vests and equipment, and personnel and vehicle search equipment. The ATBN also receives intensive training in areas related to urban warfare, raid operations, bodyguard services, countersurveillance, and nuclear, biological, chemical, and radiological environments.

MARINE EXPEDITIONARY UNIT (MEU)

The MEU is considered to be the basic building block for all MAGTF operations. These units are designed to be the Marine Corps' first-on-the-scene force—a so-called "911 Band-Aid." As such, MEUs are embarked aboard U.S. Navy ships, where they continuously patrol the Mediterranean Sea, the western Pacific, and the Indian Ocean or Persian Gulf region. These 1,500- to 3,000-strong task forces provide forward-deployed units that can conduct a variety of fast-response missions, including *in extremis* hostage rescue, evacuation, humanitarian aid, tactical recovery of personnel, clandestine reconnaissance, intelligence collection, specialized demolitions, and seizure of airports or offshore platforms.

Under the command of a colonel and equipped with 15 days of supplies, an MEU is made up of a reinforced infantry battalion, a composite aviation squadron (for example, 20 helicopters and 6 AV-8B Harriers), and a service support group (including such components as motor transport, military police, and landing support). The MEU is heavily armed with a variety of weapon systems, including 5 M1A1 Abrams battle tanks, 8 155mm howitzers, 12 amphibious assault vehicles, 9 60mm mortars, and numerous antitank launchers.

Since MAGTF operations depend so much on the ability of the first-on-the-scene force, MEUs are among the most highly trained elements of a Marine Expeditionary Force and carry the special designator "special operations capable" (MEU/SOC). To earn this designation, each MEU undergoes a demanding 26-week predeployment training program that culminates with a multiday special operations capable exercise (SOCEX) that tests the MEU's ability to plan and execute a number of "no-notice" missions within six hours of the receipt of the alert order. It also tests the unit's ability to conduct multiple missions simultaneously. Every MEU/SOC must be tested and qualified to handle the entire spectrum of 19 different mission capabilities, ranging from amphibious raids to urban warfare.

Unlike U.S. Special Operations Command components—such as SEALs and Green Berets—the MEU/SOC is America's *only* special-operations-capable force that

Above: A Stinger surface-to-air missile is fired by Marines during training in South Korea. The fire-and-forget missile, which has a range of about 5 miles, locks on to the heat emitting from a low-altitude aircraft or helicopter. The Marines use the shoulder-fired weapon to defend forward combat areas, vital areas, and installations from enemy attack.

Right: As trained, a Marine scout-sniper team uses local vegetation to decorate their ghillie suits. The camouflaged netting/overcover is worn by snipers to prevent them from being spotted by the enemy. By carefully selecting materials that blend in with the color, texture, and vegetation of the environment he will be operating in, a sniper is nearly invisible when lying down, since there is no distinguishing human outline or tell-tale shadows.

As a sea-based force, the Marines are at home on the water, in the water and, in many instances, even under the water. Force Recon Marines routinely use open- and closed-circuit diving equipment to conduct hydrographic surveys and to insert into enemy-held territory. More recently they have worked with the Navy SEALs, including insertions using minisubs. In this photo, the *Los Angeles*–class attack submarine the USS *Greenville* (SSN-772) tests a new 65-foot-long minisub known as the Advanced SEAL Delivery System (ASDS) off the coast of Hawaii. The sub is operated by a crew of two, and it can transport eight divers, including Marines. *U.S. Navy*

lives, trains, and deploys as one unit. The Marine Corps currently has seven MEU/SOCs: the 22nd, 24th, and 26th MEUs are attached to the U.S. Marine Corps Forces Atlantic, and the 11th, 13th, 15th, and 31st MEUs are attached to the U.S. Marine Corps Forces Pacific.

Captain Scott O'Grady, the Air Force fighter pilot shot down over Bosnia, and the American citizens and foreign nationals trapped in the U.S. Embassy in Tirana, Albania, were all rescued by forward-deployed, first-on-the-scene MEU/SOCs.

SPECIAL PURPOSE MAGTF (SPMAGTF)

The smallest of all MAGTFs (100–1,000 Marines), these units are under the command of whatever officer grade is considered necessary to achieve the objective at hand. Special-purpose forces are deployed for both conventional and unconventional operations and, as such, their weapons selection and self-sustainment capability vary with the mission. They are most often organized and equipped to conduct crisis response, training exercises, and peacetime missions (such as humanitarian relief).

Helicopter crashes can occur any time, but for Marines who routinely fly aboard CH-46 and CH-53 helos over the ocean, it can be a lethal event. Since the weight of the rotors flip a helicopter upside-down after a water crash, Marines must learn how to quickly exit. This photo shows a modular amphibious egress training (MAET) simulator in action. The Marines sit inside and, after the MAET spins over, they swim out following the air bubbles to the surface.

Left: A beachmaster instructs a line of amphibious assault vehicles (AAVP7) to take a different direction down the Camp Pendleton shoreline, since that section was closed to allow LCACs to deliver Marines from amphibious ships off shore. Although the AAVP7s are bulky looking and can weight up to 60,000 pounds when loaded with cargo, earning them the nickname "hippo," they take to water like ducks. They routinely transport Marines ashore during amphibious operations, moving 6 miles per hour in the ocean and 20–30 miles per hour on land.

They are designated as SPMAGTF with a mission, location, or exercise name, such as SPMAGTF-Somalia. Due to their small size, these forces are ideal for responding covertly to crises in foreign lands, often deploying by aircraft, surface ship, and even submarine.

When a crisis arises requiring a military response, the Marine Corps can rapidly combine forces from any base location to form a composite MAGTF without worrying about whether or not they will fit together. That's because, as mentioned previously, all MAGTFs share the same organizational structure—command, ground combat, air combat, and combat service support elements. Like building blocks, the Marine Corps simply adds to whatever force is "first on the scene"—usually a MEU/SOC—until the capabilities necessary to accomplish the mission are available. The elements of smaller MAGTFs are readily absorbed into the next higher-level companion element.

This unique approach conserves military resources, while swiftly enabling the on-scene force to ratchet its

A proper "paint job" can effectively hide a Marine in the brush. All Marines are trained to use camouflage materials to reduce the possibility of being detected by enemy forces. Some rules of thumb include: darkening shine areas of the face and lightening shadow areas, using irregular patterns, removing items that reflect light, and using local vegetation to match your surroundings.

capabilities up or down. Although this building-block approach seems clear-cut, it requires detailed planning and integration, as well as:

- Highly trained, first-on-the-scene forces that are able to handle a number of tasks well
- A heavier "forcible-entry" military force that can kick open the door and hold it open—in spite of heavy enemy opposition—until follow-on forces arrive

- A flexible expansion force that is capable of rein forcing first-on-the-scene MAGTFs, to create new, more powerful MAGTFs

AIR CONTINGENCY MAGTF (ACM)

In addition to the four Marine Air-Ground Task Forces—MEF, MEB, MEU, and Special Purpose—the Marines have one *additional* surprise up their sleeve. In the event of a fast-breaking crisis, an Air Contingency MAGTF (ACM) can be sent in. It is composed of regular MEF combat and support forces that are continually on standby alert status. As long as no crisis exists, they carry on normal operations. However, when an emergency erupts and the call "Send in the Marines!" is bellowed, the forces come together and deploy as a MAGTF by strategic airlift within 18 hours of notification.

Unlike the MEU/SOC, which has the ability to force its way ashore in the face of enemy fire, an ACM requires a secure airfield to fly into. Given this, an ACM has to be correctly sized (and equipped!) for the mission, threat, and available airlift, ranging in size from a reinforced rifle company up to a regiment. As such, ACMs can be used to

bolster other first-on-the-scene military units, or serve as the lead element of a MEF.

TO THE SHORES OF TRIPOLI: EXPEDITIONARY MANEUVER WARFARE

While advances in modern technology are changing the lethality of war, the means of war itself remains the same—applied organized violence. It is through the use of violence, or the credible threat of violence, that a nation forces its enemy to do its will. Violence, therefore, is an essential element of war. While the magnitude of bloodshed, destruction, and suffering vary with each situation, the violent essence of war never changes.

As America's military "Force in Readiness," the U.S. Marine Corps is tasked with pacifying belligerent nations through a show of force or, if that fails, projecting violence by using its arsenal of weapons. Understanding that adversaries will adapt their tactics and weaponry to engage the United States where they perceive it to be weak, the Marines Corps has in recent years revised its war-fighting philosophy to embrace what is known as "expeditionary maneuver warfare."

Above: One of the Marine Corps' least known units is the Sensor Control and Management Platoon (SCAMP), which is responsible for intelligence gathering, perimeter security, and calling in artillery or aircraft fire—all through the use of remote sensors. There are only 75 SCAMPs in the entire Corps. The Marines use a variety of high-tech "spy" sensors, including those that detect seismic waves made by passing vehicles, those that sense minute changes in air temperature made by passing troops, and those that measure changes in the earth's magnetic field due to the presence of an armored vehicle. SCAMP delivers these sensors in enemy-held territory by deploying with a reconnaissance patrol or a scout-sniper team. In this photo, a SCAMP sensor operator assigned to the 22nd MEU/SOC retrieves a sensor used in a training exercise.

Left: Two amphibious assault vehicles (AAVP7) emerge from the ocean and fire their weapons during a training exercise at Luzon Island, Philippines. The AAVP7s, which transport 21 combat-equipped Marines from ship to shore, are armed with a .50-caliber machine gun and a 40mm grenade-launching machine gun. *U.S. Navy*

This way of thinking acknowledges that speed, stealth, precision, and sustainability have become increasingly important aspects of warfare. Hence, maneuver warfare stresses proactive thought and action to anticipate what the enemy is doing and to quickly counter it. It encourages decentralized decision-making, which allows Marines to exploit the chaotic nature of combat by seizing fleeting opportunity and engaging enemy forces from positions of advantage. This results in Marines outthinking, outmaneuvering, and outfighting their adversaries in all dimensions—land, air, and sea—at the time and place of their choosing.

The ultimate consequence of maneuver warfare is that the enemy's cohesion is shattered, leaving him vulnerable to attack and unable to effectively fight.

Today, the Marine Corps is developing officers who can thrive in this type of combat setting. It is seeking to produce leaders who can function in an environment of uncertainty; who exhibit traits of nerve and restraint; and who can recognize patterns, discern critical information, and make intuitive decisions quickly without having all the facts.

To initiate expeditionary maneuver warfare, the Marines rely on their relationship with the Navy to use the sea as maneuver space and as a protected base from which they can project power anywhere in the world. By operating from warships at sea, the Marines can respond quickly to a crisis and maintain a presence in an area almost indefinitely, while eliminating the need for ground-based staging. A self-contained MEU/SOC—along with attack aircraft, naval guns, and sea-launched cruise missiles—can bob on the ocean within sight of a belligerent nation's coast and make its citizens think twice about picking a fight.

U.S. ARMED FORCES CODE OF CONDUCT

Article I
I am an American, fighting in the forces which guard my country and our way of life. I am prepared to give my life in their defense.

Article II
I will never surrender of my own free will. If in command, I will never surrender the members of my command while they still have the means to resist.

Article III
If I am captured, I will continue to resist by all means available. I will make every effort to escape and to aid others to escape. I will accept neither parole nor special favors from the enemy.

Article IV
If I become a prisoner of war, I will keep faith with my fellow prisoners. I will give no information nor take part in any action which might be harmful to my comrades. If I am senior, I will take command. If not, I will obey lawful orders of those appointed over me and will back them in every way.

Article V
When questioned, should I become a prisoner of war, I am required to give name, rank, service number, and date of birth. I will evade answering further questions to the utmost of my ability. I will make no oral or written statements disloyal to my country or its allies, or harmful to their cause.

Article VI
I will never forget that I am an American, fighting for freedom, responsible for my actions, and dedicated to the principles which made my country free. I will trust in my God and in the United States of America.

The Marine Corps is becoming more involved with low-intensity conflict and riot control when deployed overseas. To prepare for this growing mission profile, Marines in this photo are training with Naval Security personnel at Camp Garcia on Vieques Island, Puerto Rico. Camp Garcia's main mission is to support joint task force exercises and training missions of the U.S. Atlantic Fleet. *U.S. Navy*

It takes the strength of three Marines to load a 155mm artillery round into the M198 howitzer.

A Marine assigned to the 26th MEU/SOC and deployed at Kandahar, Afghanistan, carefully positions his M249 machine gun for the evening security watch. The 5.56mm weapon, which is the basis for a fire team, is used to engage targets out to 2,400 feet. The gunner has the option of using 30-round magazines or linked ammunition from a preloaded 200-round magazine. *U.S. Navy*

Speed is vital on the battlefield, whether attacking the enemy or, as shown in this photo, getting away from an amphibious assault vehicle (AAVP7) before the enemy can shoot you. Exiting a combat vehicle is always the most hazardous moment for a Marine. To lessen the risk of being shot outright, the AAVP7 has its infantry compartment door at the rear. This allows the driver and gunner to position the vehicle toward the enemy and engage them with heavy weapons fire while the Marines quickly deploy. *U.S. Navy*

Marines from the 31st MEU/SOC fast-rope out of the rear of a CH-46 Sea Knight helicopter while participating in a training exercise. Fast-roping is similar to sliding down a fire pole, only the thick rope moves not only with the helicopter's motion but also with the downward rotor wash. Many Marines liken fast-roping to a controlled fall. *U.S. Navy*

An 81mm mortar crew assigned to the 22nd MEU/SOC duck after firing a round down range during a live-fire training exercise at Camp Lejeune. The M252 mortar weighs about 89 pounds, and has an extended range of 15,000 feet. It can fire a maximum of 33 rounds per minute.

In the past, American naval forces deployed in two major configurations—aircraft carrier battle groups (CVBGs) and amphibious ready groups (ARGs). Battle groups represented the primary striking force of the fleet, embracing 10 warships, 2 nuclear attack submarines, a replenishment ship, 13,000 sailors, and an air wing of 70 aircraft. It was capable of waging war in a number of different and unique arenas, including electronic warfare, antisubmarine warfare, antiair warfare, surface warfare, air strikes, combat air patrols, and reconnaissance.

The ARGs comprised three or four amphibious ships (also called "gators") and 2,200 combat-ready Marines of a MEU/SOC. Since they were not accompanied by surface warships or submarines, the ARGs had to wait in-theater for the arrival of a battle group before initiating combat operations. They needed the availability of the battle group's high-volume, all-weather gunfire for suppression, area denial, and harassment missions. They also needed intelligence information to maintain situational awareness, identify targets, and assess the enemy's intent and capabilities. And they needed the protective umbrella of the battle group's powerful air wing to keep the enemy at bay.

With the emergence of the Global War on Terrorism at the start of the twenty-first century, the Navy and Marine Corps realized that the CVBG/ARG concept was no longer adequate. The battlefield was quickly metamorphosing into an environment requiring a highly flexible and responsive military force. By the time a battle group arrived to support an ARG (or vice versa), the combatants were long gone—hidden in the mountains, melted into urban centers and other locales, or dismantled entirely.

And so the Global Concept of Operations (CONOPS) was developed. It enables the United States to maintain credible deterrent forces in key areas of the world, such as the Persian Gulf, while providing military commanders with small-but-lethal task groups that can quickly respond to local or regional conflicts. It achieves this by eliminating the battle groups and ARGs, and reorganizing the naval fleet into carrier strike groups (CSG), expeditionary strike

In this early-morning look at the stern of the amphibious assault ship USS *Essex* (LHD-2) as it sits stationed off the coast of Luzon, Philippines, Marines of the 31st MEU/SOC are preparing to go ashore in a mock amphibious assault, using LCACs and other landing craft. *U.S. Navy*

MARINE SNIPER:
THE ORIGINAL "POINT AND CLICK"

Sniper. The word instills fear in even the most battle-hardened soldier. That's because it's one thing to be killed in an anonymous hail of bullets in the heat of combat, but it's entirely different when it is a single bullet that is purposely fired by an unseen assassin who patiently stalks you. Throughout history, snipers have calmly shot men dead who were eating, swimming, enjoying a drink, or emptying their bladder. That seeming callousness has a tremendous psychological impact not only on individual soldiers, but on entire armies.

A sniper may be respected by other Marines for his skills, but he can not expect to be popular. That's because warriors can accept machine-gun fire and artillery shrapnel—and even hand-to-hand combat—but they are uneasy with the thought of an unseen sniper singling them out with a bullet to the head.

Knowing that sniping dramatically influences the outcome of a battle, the Marine Corps has invested much effort in training its Scout-Snipers. As a result, the Corps has established a reputation as having the best snipers in the world. In fact, the most renowned is Gunnery Sergeant Carlos Hathcock, with 93 confirmed kills during the Vietnam conflict. Among his many legendary achievements was the methodical destruction of an entire North Vietnamese Army (NVA) company over the course of five days, as well as his three-day stalk of an NVA general.

All Marine Scout-Snipers go through a two-month-long course. The first month is largely dedicated to marksmanship, while the second month focuses on concealment, stalking, and land navigation. To become a qualified sniper, a candidate must hit a stationary target at 1,000 yards and a moving target at 800 yards 80 percent of the time or better.

The demanding course has a 40 percent drop-out rate, making it one of the toughest schools in the military.

Only the best Marines are trained as snipers. Among the many traits sought are:
- Mental and emotional stability: the ability to remain calm under stress
- Good physical fitness and stamina
- Patience, maturity, and intelligence
- Expert marksman
- Confidence with map and compass
- Knowledge of woodcraft
- Decisive, intuitive thinking
- Methodical nature
- Ability to be employed independently
- Good observation skills

Marine snipers presently use the M40A1 bolt-action 7.62 x 51mm rifle (soon to be replaced by the M40A3) that is "tricked-out" with a competition-grade stainless steel barrel, fiberglass stock, modified trigger, five-round magazine, and a 10x Unertl scope whose lenses are coated with a high-efficiency, low-reflection film that enables the scope to gather 91 percent of the available light. By comparison, in an uncoated lens 45 percent of the light is lost. This makes the rifle extremely accurate, enabling the sniper to hit targets at up to 1,000 yards, even in low-light situations.

Snipers are also skilled in using the powerful M82 Barrett .50-caliber semiautomatic rifle as an antiarmor weapon. The 37.5-pound weapon is often deployed with Force Recon in three-man fire teams, and is used to disrupt communications, disable vehicles and aircraft, knock out radar and other material targets, and kill personnel at distances in excess of a mile.

Marines undergoing sniper training (as well as members from other military services and the FBI) receive instruction not only in sniping but also in infantry tactics, camouflage, tracking and countertracking, map and aerial photo reading, and land navigation. They also are trained in communications, insertion and extraction techniques, outdoor survival skills, and supporting arms fire. They learn that patience is the essence of sniping. That's because a sniper, who is usually dressed in a camouflaged ghillie suit to blend in with the environment, moves only feet and inches at a time—typically for days on end—until he is finally in position to fire a single, lethal shot at the target from a concealed location. During that time, he endures irritating bug bites, weather extremes, sleep deprivation, constipation, and cuts and blisters caused by slithering over, under, and through rough terrain.

The students are constantly reminded by instructors that they only get one opportunity—and usually, just one shot—to hit a target: hence, the adage "One shot, one kill." To fire twice enables the enemy to pinpoint his location. That's because a rifle makes two noises when fired—the sharp crack of the bullet being shot, and the dull thump of the report. Someone who hears both can determine not only the general direction from which the noise was made, but also the distance. The closer the crack and thump occur together, the closer the sniper.

Marine snipers learn to be deployed in the field in pairs. The sniper fires the rifle while the scout (who is also a trained sniper) uses a 20-power scope to acquire targets, conduct surveillance, and estimate range. Through the scope, the spotter can track the bullet's path, because it creates a wake as it displaces the air, much as a boat creates a wake. If the sniper misses with his first shot, the spotter can make a quick correction. The sniper and scout trade roles about every half-hour to avoid fatigue.

Combat missions generally require the sniper team to assume one of two roles: to deliver precise fire at targets from long distances and from a concealed location and to conduct surveillance in support of a military operation. The snipers are trained to shoot targets that influence the outcome of armed conflict, such as officers, crew-served weapons such as machine guns and artillery, senior NCOs, snipers, communications, and observation sensors.

Once a Marine passes the intense two-month-long course, he is qualified to be assigned to a Scout-Sniper Platoon in a MEU/SOC or other unit. Such a platoon is made up of three Scout Sniper Squads, each of which consists of a squad leader (who generally holds the rank of sergeant), five sniper team leaders (corporal), and five scout-observers (lance corporal).

A sniper's M40A1 rifle is built from stock parts by the armorers of the Weapons Training Battalion at Quantico. All snipers shoot Lake City M118 match-grade 7.62mm ammunition (173-grain boat-tail bullet with a velocity of 2,550 feet per second) because it consistently provides the same expected results. If other 7.62mm ammo is used, the sniper cannot count on anticipated bullet drop, velocity, or point of impact.

groups (ESG), surface action groups (SAG), and independently operating guided-missile submarines (SSGN).

In this reorganization, the Marine Corps' MEU/SOC combat task forces are embarked in the expeditionary strike groups, which now consist of amphibious ships of the old ARG plus several surface warships and submarines, including:

- Amphibious Assault Ship, *Tarawa* and *Wasp* classes)—The primary amphibious landing ships designed to put Marines on hostile shores using LCAC hovercraft and other landing craft. The aircraft carrier-like flight deck supports AV-8B Harrier jets, attack helicopters, and antisubmarine warfare helicopters.
- Amphibious Transport Dock (*San Antonio* and *Austin* classes)—An amphibious ship that transports and land elements of a Marine landing force using landing craft
- Dock Landing Ship (*Harpers Ferry* and *Whidbey Island* classes)—An amphibious ship that transports and lands elements of a Marine landing force using LCAC hover craft and other landing craft

- Guided Missile Cruiser (*Ticonderoga* class)—A multimission surface warship equipped with Tomahawk cruise missiles for long-range strikes
- Guided Missile Destroyer (*Arleigh Burke* class)—A multimission surface warship used primarily in the antiaircraft role
- Frigate (*Oliver Hazard Perry* class)—A surface warship used primarily in the antisubmarine role
- Attack Submarine (*Los Angeles, Seawolf,* and *Virginia* classes)—Used to seek out and destroy hostile surface warships and submarines
- In some instances, land-based P-3C Orion antisubmarine warfare aircraft can be assigned to an ESG to patrol the oceans for enemy submarines.

The inclusion of the surface warships and fast-attack submarines give the ESG greater mobility, lethality, and enhanced defensive capabilities when at sea, as well as more striking power in the form of Tomahawk cruise missiles and naval gunfire. With it, the MEU/SOC does not have to wait to "kick 100 percent Marine whoop-ass." Its "posse" is always with them.

The Marines conduct the first-ever joint-amphibious landing with Russian, Polish, and Lithuanian forces in Ustka, Poland.

A Marine in a LAV-25 prepares to move out on night patrol near Kandahar, Afghanistan. The green-colored tubes behind him eject smoke and flares to protect the vehicle from attack. The smoke can obscure the enemy's vision, while a hot flare can distract an incoming heat-seeking missile. *U.S. Navy*

To maintain their marksmanship when at sea for long periods of time, the Marines often set up targets on the flight deck of the amphibious assault ship for a bit of shooting practice. Here, the target is Osama bin Laden, whom the Marines of the 2nd Marine Expeditionary Brigade hope to hunt down. As one favorite Marine bumper sticker reads: "It's God's job to forgive bin Laden, it's our job to arrange the meeting." *U.S. Navy*

"Here, kitty, kitty." All jesting aside, survival skills play an important role in keeping a Marine alive when out in the field. That includes knowing how to handle dangerous snakes, such as this cobra. While at Camp S. D. Butler in Okinawa, undergoing jungle survival training, this Force Recon Marine learned to safely catch and pick up the snake. The trick is to slowly move the hand to the back of the cobra's head, and then gently push the head down to the ground in order to grab its neck.

WAR IN RESERVE

To speed the process of deploying the Marines to the battlefield, the Navy's Military Sealift Command has anchored 16 T-AK designated cargo ships at strategic locations around the world. Known as the Maritime Prepositioning Force (MPF), these three squadrons, each composed of four to six merchant vessels, are located at Diego Garcia (Indian Ocean), Guam/Saipan (Western Pacific), and in the western Mediterranean—where they are no more than 7 to 14 days sailing time from a possible flashpoint. Each squadron contains enough weapons, vehicles, ammunition, fuel, water, and 30 days of provisions to equip a Marine Expeditionary Brigade (MEB) totaling about 18,000 Marines—until supplies can be shipped from the continental United States.

The cargo holds of all ships are temperature and humidity controlled. A small civilian crew is assigned to each vessel to regularly check the supplies and to perform routine maintenance. Every 2 1/2 years, each ship returns to Jacksonville, Florida, to have its cargo unloaded, inspected, and repaired or replaced.

During Operation Iraqi Freedom in 2003, two of the three MPF squadrons—11 ships total—were unloaded in the Persian Gulf to support the Marine Corps with tanks, vehicles, and equipment. Following the war, a special purpose MAGTF of about 2,000 Marines was given the responsibility of bringing the equipment used in combat back up to a usable condition and reloading it aboard the prepositioning ships. That way the MPFs would be ready to respond immediately to another crisis.

The MPF squadrons are loaded in such a way that individual ships can be selectively off-loaded to support smaller missions. For example, one ship in each squadron is earmarked to augment a MEU/SOC, while other ships carry supplies for humanitarian operations. Still other ships are equipped to support MAGTFs involved in low-intensity conflicts, such as guerilla warfare and counterterrorism operations.

Under the MPF premise, Marines from a MEB are flown by up to 120 cargo planes (e.g., C-5 Galaxy, C-141 StarLifter, C-17 Globemaster) directly to the area of conflict. There, they unite with the maritime prepositioning ships and then either begin military operations or reinforce a MEU/SOC that is already on the ground. The incoming Marines are expected to be combat ready within five days of meeting up with the MPF.

The ultimate usefulness of the Maritime Prepositioning Force is its flexibility. Through a building-block approach, the squadrons provide commanders with an extremely rapid means of projecting military power anywhere on earth.

In the event of a serious conflict, all three MPF squadrons can be merged to support a Marine Expeditionary Force, the Marine Corps' largest warfighting team. This is exactly what happened during Operation Desert Shield/Desert Storm. The entire MPF unloaded its cargo in Saudi Arabia for use by all combat forces beginning in mid-August 1990. And during Operation Iraqi Freedom in 2003, two MPF squadrons—11 ships total—were unloaded in the Persian Gulf to support the Marine Corps. Following the war, a special purpose MAGTF of about 2,000 Marines was given the responsibility of bringing the equipment used in combat back up to a usable condition, and reloading it aboard the prepositioning ships. That way the MPFs would be ready to respond immediately to another crisis.

In fact, forward-deployed expeditionary strike groups are designed to respond immediately to crises (or military opportunities) in six hours' time. Additionally, the ESGs can cover 75 percent of the littoral regions of the world within five days. (It is worth noting that nearly 80 percent of the world's population lives within 200 miles of the ocean.) As for the MEU/SOC, wherever it is deployed, it has a direct impact on a 6,000-square-mile area. But if you consider the Tomahawk Land-Attack Missile, that area grows to an incredible 360,000 square miles.

Under Global CONOPS, there eventually will be 37 independent strike groups to project power abroad: 12 carrier strike groups, 12 expeditionary strike groups, 9

Like marksmanship skills, hand-to-hand combat skills can be easily lost if not practiced routinely. And if you're in a combat zone like Iraq, those are skills you do not want to become rusty. In this photo, a Marine delivers a hammer fist to the other's chest during a martial arts session. The training was conducted during the predawn hours to avoid the hot desert heat, which soared to 110 degrees by 0900 hours.

The Marine Corps not only fights wars, it fights diseases, too. In this photo, a civil affairs team crosses a swift river to assist in vaccinating 15,000 children in eastern Ethiopia from polio. The week-long journey had them crossing mountains and extremely tough terrain, but the Humvee held up like a champ.

Chemical, Biological Incident Response Force (CBIRF) Marines, as part of Operation Noble Eagle, the homeland defense campaign initiated in September 2001, move decontamination gear away from the hot zone established around the Dirksen Senate Office Building in the fall of 2001. A 100-man initial response force based at nearby Indian Head, Maryland, responded after anthrax was discovered inside the building. They collected more than 600 biological samples and removed and screened 12 tons of congressional mail and office equipment.

Members of the 1st Fleet Antiterrorism Security Team (FAST), 4th Platoon, deploy from the commander of the Seventh Fleet's helicopter during an exercise aboard the command-and-control ship USS *Blue Ridge* (LCC-19). FAST is responsible for providing special security, rescuing hostages, and containing terrorists.

As part of a 3-mile endurance course while at the Jungle Warfare Training Center at Camp Gonsalves in Okinawa, Marines must conduct a hasty rappel, face-first (also called the Australian rappel) down the side of a cliff. As part of the intense training, the so-called "Lava Dog" Marines learn jungle shooting and patrolling, rough terrain movement, and survival skills.

Since the Marine Corps fights in all climes and places, it trains for snowy and inclement weather fighting at its Mountain Warfare Training center in Bridgeport, California. Known as "Pickle Meadows," the center trains Marines to survive, maneuver, and fight in prolonged, cold weather mountain operations. Training takes place at altitudes up to 8,500 feet and in temperatures below freezing. During the summer months, the center focuses on mountaineering skills, such as rappelling, mountain navigation, rock climbing, and swift-water rescue. In this photo, a Marine carries a simulated casualty during a long-range patrol exercise.

missile defense surface action groups, and 4 guided-missile submarine/special operations forces strike groups (SSGN/SOF). The latter are *Ohio*-class nuclear ballistic-missile submarines that, since 2003, have been gutted and refitted to provide covert striking power with cruise missiles and the clandestine insertion of special operations forces. The submarines can carry and support a team of 66 Navy SEAL and Marine Force recon operators for up to 90 days, as compared to 15 days for a team inserted by a fast-attack submarine. The four converted submarines are the USS *Ohio*, the USS *Florida*, the USS *Michigan,* and the USS *Georgia*. Each can launch up to 154 Tomahawk missiles, as well as unmanned reconnaissance vehicles and the new 65-foot-long Advanced SEAL Delivery System, a minisub that transports eight combatants.

These 37 strike groups will operate throughout the world to address threats to America's interests. When it appears that a regional conflict is inevitable, they will join together, along with the Maritime Prepositioning Force, to create a naval strike force that a commander-in-chief can direct to wage war.

The first expeditionary strike group—ESG-1 with the USS *Peleliu* (LHA-5) assuming the role of command ship—was established in 2002. It was the first ESG to be deployed under the Global CONOPS, entering the U.S. Central Command's area of authority in the Arabian Gulf in September 2003 in support of Operation Iraqi Freedom. In addition to the *Peleliu*, the San Diego-based group consists of the USS *Germantown* (LSD-42), the USS *Odgen* (LPD-5), the USS *Port Royal* (CG-73), the USS *Decatur* (DDG-73), the USS *Jarret* (FFG-33), and the fast-attack submarine USS *Greenville* (SSN-772). The 13th MEU/SOC was embarked aboard the gators and provided a postwar presence in the region, aided in peacekeeping, and promoted an environment conducive to building the new Iraqi government. The group also conducted searches of vessels in the Arabian Gulf to prevent the smuggling of oil. ESG-1 returned to the United States after its six-month deployment in March 2004.

ESG-2, whose home port is Norfolk, Virginia, was established in late 2003 with the USS *Wasp* (LHD-1) serving as the flagship. The 22nd MEU/SOC is assigned to this strike group, which consists of the USS *Yorktown* (CG-48), the USS *Leyte Gulf* (CG-55), the USS *McFaul* (DDG-74), the USS *Shreveport* (LPD-12), the USS *Whidbey Island* (LSD-41), and the new attack submarine USS *Connecticut* (SSN-22).

At the time of this writing, ESG-3 has been established with the USS *Belleau Wood* (LHA-3) as flagship—with a Marine colonel as commander—and with the 11th MEU/SOC embarked. Both ESG-4 and ESG-5 are in the process of being formulated, most likely around the USS *Essex* (LHD-2) and the USS *Saipan* (LHA-2).

A medic must not only know emergency medicine to aid wounded Marines, but he must also know how to survive on the battlefield, since he deploys with Marine units. To ensure that a medic is worthy of accompanying them, the Marines themselves provide the combat training, including movement and patrolling techniques, and how to make an entrenchment. In this photo, the medics learn what it's like to be wet and dirty, as well as what bugs and slimy things look like up close.

FOUR

An LCAC (also called "Hopper" and "Flying Carpet") rushes up onto Onslow Beach at Camp Lejeune in North Carolina at 15 knots, carrying a payload weighing up to 70 tons. Amphibious-assault training exercises, such as this one, mimic real world combat conditions as much as possible, heeding the advice: Train as you fight. *S. F. Tomajczyk*

Amphibious Assault

Forward deployed forces, primarily naval expeditionary forces—the Navy-Marine Corps team—are vital to regional stability and to keeping crises from escalation into full-scale wars. To those who argue that the United States cannot afford to have this degree of vigilance any more, we say: The United States can't afford not to.
Admiral Jay Johnson, Chief of Naval Operations
General Charles C. Krulak, 31st Commandant of the Marine Corps

We're Marines. We took Iwo Jima. Baghdad ain't shit.
General John Kelly, USMC

It is 0330 hours and the aircraft hangar of the amphibious assault ship the USS *Bataan* (LHD-5) is filled with hundreds of heavily armed Marines busily checking their rifles and painting their faces in shades of green. They are preparing for combat, and the air is filled with tension. In the level immediately below them, the flooded well deck is drowning in the high-pitched noise of three idling air-cushioned LCACs, which will transport the Marines and their equipment to enemy beaches located over the horizon.

Meanwhile, on the *Bataan's* dark flight deck, the CH-46E Sea Knight and CH-53E Super Stallion helicopters are revving up, their cargo space filled with a Marine attack element. Their mission is to take over an enemy-held airport several miles inland from the beach. They will be protected from the air by AV-8B Harrier jump jets and AH-1W Super Cobra attack helicopters, which are also in the last stages of preparation to fly off the *Bataan*.

The *Bataan* is not the only ship that is busy at this early morning hour. Close by, aboard the USS *Whidbey Island* (LSD-41) and the USS *Shreveport* (LPD-12), Marines are busy loading their LAV-25s, Humvees, 155mm howitzers, and personal gear aboard LCACs and other landing craft.

If all goes well, the airport will be taken and the first wave of Marines will land on the beach before the sun rises, just 1 1/2 hours from now. This is the intense and noisy world of amphibious warfare.

THE PRINCESS GATOR

If the aircraft carrier is the queen of the Navy's surface fleet, then the amphibious assault ship is the princess, and centerpiece, of the newly created expeditionary strike group. Resembling a smaller version of an aircraft carrier, the amphibious assault ship transports Marines and their combat equipment ashore, using helicopters and air-cushioned landing craft (LCAC). Its secondary role is to use AV-8B Harrier attack jets and antisubmarine warfare helicopters to perform sea-control and limited power-projection missions.

Two types of amphibious assault ships bring the Marines to the world's maritime sandboxes: the *Tarawa*-class, designated LHAs, and the *Wasp*-class, designated LHDs. Each of the five *Tarawa*-class ships accommodates a detachment of 1,900 Marines. It features extensive command and communications facilities, 3 operating rooms and 300 beds for wounded Marines, a special 5,000-square-foot room that allows Marines to exercise in a controlled environment similar to that in which they will be deployed, about 30,000 square feet of vehicle storage space, and 110,000 cubic feet of cargo storage space.

The ships stern docking well, which measures 268 feet in length and 78 feet in width, can accommodate the following landing craft arrangements: 4 LCU-1610s, or 3

Three fully loaded LCACs patiently wait in the USS *Bataan's* well deck. In just a few moments, the stern gate will drop and the *Bataan* will sink eight feet to allow the landing craft to back out and head for shore. Before the LCACs start their engines, side doors along the length of the well deck will be opened to vent the exhaust and to keep the ship's hull from being overpressurized. The red lighting scheme is used to preserve the LCAC crew's night vision, as the assault will begin at 0430 hours. Note the cabin ("cockpit") to the left. It houses the four-man LCAC crew. *S. F. Tomajczyk*

At 0400 hours in the below-deck hangar of the USS *Bataan*, hundreds of armed Marines from the 22nd MEU/SOC prepare to head for the beach aboard landing craft. The Marines are grouped by the assault wave they will be participating in. There are approximately seven waves, each tasked with transporting specific equipment. Note that although the *Bataan* is large enough to carry upward of 40 aircraft, space is at a premium—as evident by the aircraft fuel pods suspended from the ceiling. As for the high-contrast yellow lighting, it is used in the hangar area so that debris—which might contaminate a jet engine—is easier to spot and remove. *S. F. Tomajczyk*

Marines of the 22nd MEU/SOC rush ashore before dawn in the first wave of an amphibious assault that took place at Camp Lejeune during a joint task force exercise. This beach is supposedly located in the fictitious nation of Kartuna. Note that two LCACs performed a side-to landing, by turning the crafts so they are parallel to the ocean. This allows vehicles to exit the landing craft and drive onto hard-packed sand without getting stuck. In this photo, two M1A1 Abrams main battle tanks, a Humvee, and a LAV-25 head inland as part of the assault team. *S. F. Tomajczyk*

Two LAV-25s, parked along side one another, pull some down time during an exercise at Camp Lejeune, enabling the Marines to relax, chat, and do some strategizing. The eight-wheeled vehicle has a crew of three and can carry six additional Marines. The Marines sit three to a side in the cargo area, and fire their weapons through ports. The eerie-looking forest in the background was not caused by artillery but, rather, by Mother Nature. Camp Lejeune is often hit by powerful hurricanes, which strip the leaves and small branches off the trees. *S. F. Tomajczyk*

105

LCM-8s and 2 LCUs, or 17 LCM-6s, or 45 amphibious assault vehicles. Generally, only 1 LCAC can be carried.

As for aircraft, *Tarawa*-class gators typically carry 16 CH-46 Sea Knight and CH-53 Sea Stallion cargo helicopters, 4 AH-1W Super Cobra attack helicopters, 3 UH-1N Huey command and control helos, and 6 AV-8B Harrier Vertical/Short Takeoff and Landing (V/STOL) jump jets. The ships are armed with 4 25mm machine guns, 3 .50-caliber machine guns, 2 20mm Phalanx CIWS (close-in weapon system) Gatling-style guns, and 2 rolling airframe missile launchers, an advanced short-range,

fire-and-forget missile used against enemy aircraft and incoming missiles.

The *Wasp* class (LHD 1) began entering service in 1989, with the latest ship—the *Makin Island* (LHD-8)—presently under construction for delivery in 2007. These ships, the largest amphibious ships in the world, are similar to the *Tarawa*-class, except they have less vehicle and cargo storage space, carry more aircraft and LCACs, and have relocated vital command and communications facilities deep into the hull for better protection against enemy attack.

With afterburners glowing white from being set at "military thrust," a Marine F/A-18 Hornet roars off the bow of the USS *John F. Kennedy*. Today's catapults could toss a full-size Cadillac sedan more than half a mile; the problem is finding a driver. This power is necessary to get a fully loaded fighter airborne in just 300 feet. The United States is one of the few nations in the world that has the technical and industrial skill to build catapults. *S. F. Tomajczyk*

Left: In the predawn hours at Camp Lejeune, an M1A1 Abrams main battle tank races over the sand at 30 miles per hour after being brought ashore from an amphibious ship by an LCAC. This highly mobile tank has a 120mm smoothbore main gun that can hit targets 12,000 feet away with kinetic-energy (sabot) and chemical-energy rounds. Its onboard sensors and computers automatically adjust the fire to account for tank movement, wind speed, temperature, and target lead. The tank features both an NBC overpressure protection system and an improved armor package to protect its crew of four. It is also equipped with a .50-caliber and two 7.62mm machine guns. The Abrams is compatible with all amphibious ships, landing craft, and maritime prepositioning ships. *S. F. Tomajczyk*

Right: The business end of an AH-1W Super Cobra attack helicopter presents a narrow profile that makes it extremely agile and difficult to hit with enemy weapon fire. The Cobra's bite can include a 20mm turreted cannon with 750 rounds, and its four external wing stations can fire 2.75-inch and 5-inch rockets, TOW and Hellfire antiarmor missiles, Sidewinder antiaircraft missiles, and Sidearm antiradar missiles. The AH-1W's missions include armed escort, air defense, and armed/visual reconnaissance. It routinely provides fire support to the landing force during an amphibious assault. In this photo, the Cobra is refueling at a forward operating base in Iraq during Operation Iraqi Freedom.

As the saying goes, "Where there's smoke, there's fire," which is why the Marines bailed out of this injured AAVP7 on Onslow Beach at Camp Lejeune. Fortunately, the Marine Corps' amphibious assault planners anticipate that a certain percentage of combat vehicles will go out of service during a landing and make plans accordingly to retrieve and repair them. In the meanwhile, the affected Marines are spirited forward by other vehicles to their original objective. *S. F. Tomajczyk*

The typical *Wasp*-class ship deploys with 1,894 Marines, as well as 12 CH-46 Sea Knight and 4 CH-53 Sea Stallion transport helicopters, 6 AV-8B Harriers, 4 AH-1W Super Cobra attack helos, and 3 UH-1N Huey command and control helicopters. It is armed with 2 eight-cell NATO Sea Sparrow antiship missile launchers, 2 rolling airframe missile launchers, 3 or 4 25mm machine guns, 4 .50 caliber machine guns, and 2 or 3 20mm Phalanx CIWS.

Landing craft exit via a stern well deck that can accommodate three LCACs. Since the *Wasp*-class ships have a relatively flat-bottomed hull, they are notorious for their side-to-side rocking motion in heavy seas.

Both the *Tarawa*- and *Wasp*-class amphibious assault ships are the heart and soul of sea-based warfare. Under the protective naval gunfire provided by the expeditionary strike group's warships—the guided-missile destroyers and cruisers—they sail into harm's way and

to be the most sophisticated amphibious ship in the world, it was built from the keel up to support the Marine Corps' "mobility triad"—the integration of three emerging technologies that will significantly transform amphibious warfare capabilities in the decades to come. These technologies include the MV-22 Osprey tilt-rotor aircraft; the expeditionary fighting vehicle (EFV), for transporting Marines on land and from ship to shore; and the *San Antonio*-class amphibious platform. Together, they will enable the Marine Corps to strike faster, harder, and deeper into enemy territory.

Left: This is a sight rarely, if ever, seen on a true battlefield. Marine scout-sniper teams are always hidden far from their target and in locations (or "hides") not easily detected, such as in a deep thicket, in a pile of debris, on the roof of a building, or in a culvert. Once in a hide, a sniper must be patient, able to endure hours or even days of discomfort before taking a perfectly judged shot. He leaves absolutely no tell-tale signs of his presence; even human waste is bagged and packed out. *S. F. Tomajczyk*

The day comes early for Marines, especially in times of war. That's because the shooting does not end when the sun goes down. Here, a group of heavily loaded Force Recon Marines— as seen through night vision goggles—heads out to board CH-46 Sea Knight helicopters to practice an insertion mission as part of Exercise Crocodile, a joint Australian and American operation involving some 9,100 military personnel.

provide a rapid build-up of Marine combat forces ashore from over the horizon in the face of a determined enemy. But they do not do this alone. They are accompanied by other gators, which disgorge their smaller, 500- to 930-Marine detachments and equipment via landing craft, helicopters, and, if they fit within the well deck, LCAC hovercraft.

The latest addition to this group is the *San Antonio*-class (LPD-17) amphibious transport dock ship. Considered

FORCE RECON

The Navy has its SEALs and the Army its Green Berets, but most people are not aware that the Marine Corps, too, has its "best of the best"—Force Recon. These highly trained, stealthy Marines infiltrate deep inside enemy lines to gather intelligence and conduct search-and-destroy missions in support of Marine Expeditionary Force or other MAGTF operations.

Force Recon Marines keep a low profile while heading for their objective on a combat rubber reconnaissance craft during a raid exercise.

Earning the title of Force Recon Marine is an arduous process. It begins with a day-long screening event that weeds out the physically and psychologically weak. Those who pass this first step are placed in a Reconnaissance Indoctrination Platoon, whose deathly acronym, RIP, hints at the tough days ahead. For the next month they endure physical conditioning (they swim 5,000-plus meters every day) and learn basic land navigation and patrolling skills, as well as how to conduct hydrographic surveys.

Force Recon divers use both open- and closed-circuit air tanks. Using open-circuit scuba tanks, the Marines can safely dive to 130 feet, while the closed-circuit Mk. 25 LAR-V Draeger tanks limit them to just 25 feet. The benefit of closed-circuit diving is that there are no telltale bubbles being released for the enemy to detect—making it ideal for combat situations. The system scrubs the CO_2 exhaled by the diver and turns it back into breathable oxygen. The diver can remain underwater for four hours, depending on various factors.

During RIP, the candidates carry a 12-foot length of rope at all times, earning them the nickname "ropers." At any given time they must account for the rope's whereabouts, as well as be able to tie any type of knot demanded.

The RIP prepares Marines for the more challenging 56-day-long Basic Reconnaissance Course at the Amphibious Reconnaissance School. There, all Force Recon Marines receive advanced training in helo-casting (jumping from a helicopter into the water), marksmanship, beach surveillance, demolition, camouflage, concealment, close-quarters combat, outdoor survival, mountaineering, rappelling, extreme weather operations (e.g., desert, winter, jungle), inflatable-boat handling, forward artillery observation, and intelligence gathering.

As this suggests, Force Recon is not for the faint at heart. Every night is a late night, and the Marines are always wet and cold.

Upon completion of the Basic Reconnaissance Course, the Marines go on to attend Marine Combatant Dive School at Panama City, Florida, for two months, where they learn underwater combat tactics, infiltration techniques, and various reconnaissance methods. They also learn how to use both open- and closed-circuit diving equipment. This is followed by three weeks at the Army's Basic Airborne School, where they earn their paratrooper silver wings. They are subsequently assigned to a Force Recon Platoon.

Every Force Recon platoon goes through a recurring two-year training and deployment cycle, consisting of four phases, each of which lasts six months:

- *Individual Training Phase*—Marines attend specialized schools, such as Mountain Leaders Course, Pathfinder, Ranger School, Scout-Sniper, Dive Supervisor, and Military Freefall.
- *Unit Training Phase (Deep Reconnaissance)*—The focus is on team work. Training can include weapons and tactics, combat trauma, desert and mountain patrolling, long-range patrols, advanced communications, enemy weapons familiarization, and high-altitude high-opening parachuting.
- *MEU/SOC Direct Action Training Phase*—Much of this phase involves planning and executing missions the platoon may encounter when deployed. Training includes urban warfare and reconnaissance, applied explosives, and ship takedowns. The exercises are as realistic as possible, so the Marines are prepared for what the world has in store for them overseas.
- *MEU/SOC Deployment Overseas*—The platoon is prepared to immediately carry out any of the following missions:
- Amphibious reconnaissance
- Implant or retrieve sensors and beacons
- Provide guidance for incoming helicopters, landing craft, and parachutists
- Battle damage assessment
- Limited-scale raids
- Capture enemy personnel
- Other duties as assigned, such as humanitarian operations, seizure of airfields and ports, electronic warfare, security operations, and noncombatant evacuations.

A Force Recon platoon is made up of three six-man teams. Each Force Recon team consists of a team leader (usually a staff sergeant), an assistant team leader, a radio operator, and three reconnaissance scouts. The six-man size is unusual in the military, where four- and eight-man teams reign, but it is intentional. Given the fact that the team must jump, dive, or hike in with all the equipment necessary to complete a mission, fewer than six Marines cannot carry it all. Six also allows everyone adequate rest while maintaining security, and it provides the necessary firepower in the event enemy forces stumble across them.

Long-range patrols can last 10 days or more. It's a physically and mentally demanding task, since the Marines must remain concealed at all times. This necessitates moving at a pace that allows progress, but without alerting nearby wildlife, civilians, or military forces to the team's presence. That in itself requires the warriors to be alert and to control their every movement. A careless action can literally result in death.

Although Force Recon is considered to be a special operations unit, it is not presently affiliated with the U.S. Special Forces Command (SOCOM), a unified command established in 1987 that deploys America's elite special forces units (such as SEALs and Rangers) on joint operations worldwide. The Marine Corps was not included because Marine Corps brass reportedly did not want to give up a group of Marines to SOCOM's control and lose that corresponding support to a MEF or MEU/SOC. The Marine Corps is, after all, the nation's smallest military branch. Every Marine counts.

However, since the September 11 attacks, that thinking has changed. In 2003, Marine Detachment 1 (MAR DET 1) was created to see if Marines—most of them from Force Recon—could be integrated with a SEAL team under the command of SOCOM. The detachment is made up of 81 reconnaissance, intelligence, and fire-support Marines and 5 Navy corpsmen. After initially training in small teams, MAR DET 1 joined a SEAL team in October 2003 for joint training. In April 2004 they deployed overseas as a full, special-operations team.

Marines training in Fremo, Norway, take a defensive position outside their hide. Winter operations bring along their own problems, such as hypothermia and weapons seizing up. The Force Recon Marines also have to be careful that their breath vapor in the freezing air does not give away their location to alert enemy forces.

As of this writing, the first five ships of this 12-ship class are at various stages of construction, with the *San Antonio* itself expected to be commissioned for duty in 2005. These $641-million ships, which incorporate stealth technologies to reduce the enemy's ability to detect them with radar, will be capable of transporting and landing a 720-Marine detachment. They also have three vehicle stowage decks (24,600 square feet) for combat vehicles like tanks, assault vehicles and Humvees, and three cargo magazines (33,000 cubic feet) for stowing bulk cargo like food, clothing, weapons, and communications gear.

Like the so-called "princess gators," the *San Antonio*-class ships have a flight deck, but a smaller one. Still, it is large enough to accommodate two CH-53E Super Stallions, four CH-46 Sea Knights, six AH-1W Super Cobras, or two MV-22 Osprey vertical takeoff and landing aircraft.

In addition to two rolling airframe missile launchers and two CIWS for self-defense, the LPD-17 ships are the first to be equipped with the Mk. 46 gun weapon system, which includes two Bushmaster II stabilized 30mm cannons, a low-light television system, a thermal-imaging system, and a laser range finder that can target threats as

The USS *San Antonio* (LPD-17) is all decked out with bunting for her christening on July 21, 2003. She is the first of 12 amphibious ships that will join the Navy's gator fleet, replacing four classes of older ships in the process. The *San Antonio*-class is the most advanced amphib in the world, incorporating stealth technology and state-of-the-art electronics, communications, and command and control systems. Note the faceted mast structure in the photo (as well as the *Arleigh Burke* destroyer-like angles of her overall construction), which conceals the ship's sensors and antennas. It dramatically reduces the ship's radar signature. The *San Antonio* is scheduled to be commissioned in 2005. *Raytheon*

far away as 8,000 meters. They also have the space reserved, forward of the ship's bridge, for a vertical launch system that can fire 64 antiship Evolved Sea Sparrow Missiles (ESSM) or, if desired, several other types of missiles, such as the Tomahawk cruise missile.

The LPD-17 class possesses a state-of-the-art electronic-warfare suite that detects airborne and torpedo threats and automatically counters them by jamming or decoying. One of the more interesting tools is the Nulka decoy countermeasure system. It features a broadband radio-frequency emitter mounted atop a hovering rocket that creates a fake radar cross-section signal while flying away from the ship. This presents an incoming antiship missile with a much larger, and more attractive target. So it veers away from the amphib and homes in on the Nulka decoy instead. As these innovative ships join the fleet, they will permanently replace four classes of aging transport ships.

HITTING THE BEACHES

The United States has a reputation for possessing the strongest and best-trained amphibious force in the world. Since the days of World War II, when American military forces—including Marines attached to the I, III, and V Marine Amphibious Corps—took control of the Pacific by pushing the Japanese back across the ocean island-by-island, every nation has admired the power that is inherent in an amphibious assault force—and no one wants to be on the receiving end of it.

This was quite apparent during the 1991 Gulf War when Saddam Hussein and his military leaders focused their defensive efforts at preventing a U.S.-led amphibious

An LCU makes its way through the waves to the USS *Essex* (LHD-2) after participating in a simulated beach assault off the coast of North Carolina. If you look carefully at the *Essex*'s waterline, you'll note that her bow is slightly higher than the stern. That's because the stern gate has been lowered, allowing the ocean to flood the well deck so landing craft can enter. *U.S. Navy*

Above: A flight of three CH-53E Sea Knights is zipping through the air, ready to deliver 14 Marines with their combat gear. These are the only dual-rotor helicopters in America's arsenal, and they are used primarily to transport assault combat troops, supplies, and equipment during amphibious operations. If needed, Marines can fast-rope or helo-cast from the rear ramp of the helicopter; these techniques are often used by Force Recon Marines. The Sea Knight also serves as an air ambulance, capable of evacuating 15 litters and two attendants.

Above: "Can you hear me now?" Communications is the vital and timely link that binds the battlefield together for the Marines. Information that does not get through as intended can literally result in death and mayhem. For this reason, the Marine Corps—like all military services—has redundant communication systems in all bands of the electromagnetic spectrum, including HF, VHF, SHF, and satellite communications.

Left: Marines from the 3rd Marine Expeditionary Force (MEF) encounter a group of Australian soldiers playing the role of "enemy forces" and initiate battle during Exercise Crocodile in 2003. The Marines were supported by armored vehicles and tanks, as well as AH-1W Super Cobra attack helicopters. The mock battle was not decided by casualties, but by field umpires who provide guidance during the realistic training. Such exercises enhance the Marines' experience with joint operations, and hone their war-fighting skills.

assault against Iraqi shores by planting underwater mine-fields, placing obstacles thickly across the beaches, and positioning military assets toward the Persian Gulf to repel an attack. In the process, they forgot about the possibility of an end-around sweep or a rear attack. But you can't blame them for being blind: The United States went out of its way to tease and taunt them by parading its amphibious forces throughout the Gulf. It was an act of classic deception, and the Iraqis bought it hook, line, and sinker.

Although some critics declare amphibious warfare an antiquated and unneeded art—especially in a world marked by tactical missiles and heavily armed, supersonic jets—Marine Corps and Navy leaders vehemently disagree. They are quick to point out that the majority of conflicts and crises occurring since World War II have taken place in the littoral regions of the world—not deep inside a continent where standoff weapons are required. They also highlight the fact that most of the world's population centers are located within 200 miles of the coasts—easily within the range of either a carrier strike force or an expeditionary strike group. Hence, the doctrines and tactics of amphibious warfare, obviously modified and refined since World War II to incorporate the latest technologies, are more necessary now than ever.

Left: While a crewman from an assault amphibious vehicle (AAVP7) provides cover, Marines assigned to the 22nd MEU/SOC sprint for cover during a training exercise at Fort A. P. Hill in Virginia. While the Marines had prior training in the deserts surrounding Twentynine Palms, California, participating in a live-fire combined arms exercise (CAX), their experience at Fort A. P. Hill gave them better insight how to conduct raids in hilly, forested environments. They have more cover and concealment, which influences the way an assault is conducted.

Right: The EA-6B Prowler is the most powerful electronic warfare aircraft in existence. It is used to detect and jam enemy weapons' radar systems (such as surface-to-air missile launchers), as well as communications systems. Used by the Marines as well as the U.S. Navy and staffed by a crew of four, the Prowler escorts combat air patrols and provides cover to amphibious assault forces. The primary receiver antennas are located in a fairing on top of the tail known as the football, which provides all-around, long-distance coverage of enemy emitters. The jammers are located on the wing pylons and fuselage. In late 2003, the Department of the Navy authorized the development of the EA-18G electronic-attack aircraft. Carrying up to five jamming pods and armed with antiradiation missiles, it will eventually begin replacing the aging Prowlers after 2010.

COMBAT PROVERBS

Not everything a warrior learns comes from a textbook. Often times, the best advice is handed down from Marine to Marine, based on personal experiences in actual combat. Here is a brief collection of just plain ol' common-sense proverbs that have kept Marines alive and fighting on the battlefield.

- Carry lots of ammo; it's cheap life insurance. When in a fire fight, pace yourself. Otherwise you will run out of ammo—often at the worst time.

- On patrol and ambush: (1) Never stand when you can sit; (2) Never sit when you can lie down; (3) Never stay awake when you can sleep; and (4) Take a good shit whenever you can.

- Avoid being near a curious-looking object, since it will attract hostile fire. Likewise, avoid hiding near lone trees or rocks, fence corners, and other prominent landmarks.

- Never get into a fair fight. Be sneaky and always cheat.

- Find the enemy before he finds you. If you do not strike first, you will be the first struck.

- Move fast, strike hard, and finish rapidly.

- If you lose contact with the enemy, remember to look behind you.

- Wound the enemy since it takes at least one or two other soldiers to drag an injured soldier off the battlefield, thereby reducing the number of those left who can fight.

- Do not build your positions where the enemy would expect to find them.

- Use battlefield noises to conceal your movement.

- Avoid overcamouflaging your position. It is just as obvious as having no camouflage.

- Cross roads and trails at places that offer the most concealment, such as low spots, curves, bridges, or culverts.

- Never walk along the tops of hills or ridges, and avoid open areas.

- Tape two 30-round rifle magazines together in opposite directions. Doing so allows you to change magazines faster and more easily—even in the dark.

- Tape or pad your weapon and equipment so they do not rattle or get snagged.

- Only half a platoon should eat at one time, thereby allowing the other half to provide security in the event of an attack.

- If the enemy is within range, so are you.

- The enemy diversion you ignore is usually his main attack.

- The enemy nearly always mines the easy way out.

- When moving at night, stop frequently and listen. Remove your helmet so that sounds are not distorted by the helmet over your ears.

- The best time to escape is right after you are captured. First, you are in the best physical shape at that time. Second, friendly fire may cause enough confusion to allow you to escape. And third, you know the area where you were captured.

- If you hear the enemy launch an aerial flare, hit the ground behind cover while the flare is rising and before it illuminates the area. Should you find yourself in the lit area, get away quickly, since the enemy will be firing its weapons into that zone.

- If you must whisper, exhale most of the air from your lungs before doing so. It eliminates the tell-tale hissing that is made by a whisper.

A 40mm grenade is launched by a Marine at a training facility in Thailand as part of a counterattack exercise. The single-shot M203 launcher is fitted just under the barrel of the M16 service rifle. It is capable of firing several types of low-velocity 40mm ammunition, including fragmentation and illumination rounds.

Below: The Australian night sky is lit up by Marines from the 4th Light Armored Reconnaissance Battalion during a night-fire exercise at the Shoalwater Bay Training Area. To help mark the intended targets in the darkness, the Marines simply placed the thermal packets that normally heat their MREs near the targets so their weapons' heat-sensing scopes could detect them, providing an accurate aiming point.

Above: Watching Marines load and fire an M198 155mm howitzer is like watching a carefully orchestrated ballet. Each Marine has a specific function to make certain the artillery round is fired quickly and on target. Once a rhythm has been established, a good artillery battery can fire four rounds per minute.

So how does the United States conduct an amphibious assault? While it varies depending on the situation, there is an accepted approach that will be explored here.

The first step, as is so common in all military operations, is to collect intelligence. Yes, the military commanders of an ESG need to know where the enemy is positioned, how strong its forces are, and what it is doing, but they also need more important information. What's more important than knowing what the enemy is doing? Well, such things as the underwater topography, water depth, strength and direction of the current, seafloor slope, underwater obstacles, the compactness of the beach sand, shoreline obstacles, and enemy defenses—both above and below water. Remember, an amphibious assault means that Marines are being transported over the horizon from ship to shore. Anything and everything about the landing area must be known to prevent landing craft from hitting a mine, running aground, or entering an enemy kill zone.

Right: This is what the future of warfare will look like: Force Recon Marines are inserting by parachute from the MV-22 Osprey tilt-rotor aircraft. Force Recon Marines are trained in both HAHO (High Altitude, High Opening) and HALO (High Altitude, Low Opening) parachute techniques. They attend initial training at Fort Bragg, North Carolina, and then do the parachute jumps at Yuma, Arizona. Military freefall is used to insert small recon teams deep behind enemy lines. By using HAHO, an entire platoon can be inserted from 25,000 or more feet (breathing from oxygen bottles) from more than 24 miles away from its landing point. The MV-22 Osprey, with its ability to fly low and fast over long distances, will have a tremendous impact on covert operations. The Marines intend to acquire 360 Ospreys. Testing of the aircraft resumed in 2003 following an April 2000 crash that killed 19 Marines near Marana, Arizona.

Left: Two CH-46 Sea Knights and a UH-60Q air-ambulance Black Hawk land on a remote road near Jalibah, Iraq, during Operation Iraqi Freedom to refuel before continuing their mission northward. This refueling point was carefully selected to refuel these types of helicopters in a fast-paced environment. Logistics often plays a more important role in warfare than most are willing to admit. Without food, fuel, and ammunition, a combat force can literally fall apart.

Above: The pilot may actually fly the bird, but arguably the most important person aboard a CH-46 Sea Knight is the crew chief (front hatch in this photo). The helicopter doesn't take off (or land) until he gives the go-ahead. He is responsible for the safety of every passenger and the members of the crew. That means he checks seatbelts and ensures that gear is properly stowed away. He also keeps a sharp eye on the surroundings outside the helicopter for things that could prove dangerous, such as telephone poles, high-power electrical lines, bird flocks, and buildings. In a pinch, he can serve as a gunner and operate the helo's side-mounted machine gun. *U.S. Navy*

Above: Marines patrol in Rashid, Iraq, during Operation Iraqi Freedom to apprehend suspected organizers of an attack on coalition forces. For safety's sake, the lightly armored vehicles and Marines are spaced out, with the Marines intentionally using the LAV-25s as protection from small-arms fire.

Left: The Marines have landed . . . again. Two amphibious assault vehicles (AAVP7s) crawl onto the beach below Mount Suribachi on the island of Iwo Jima to commemorate the anniversary of the World War II battle in which Marines raised the U.S. flag atop the hill after 36 days of bloody fighting. The event inspired the famous statue that stands next to Arlington National Cemetery. *U.S. Navy*

Left: To help control forces on the battlefield, the Marine Corps relies on its UH-1N airborne command-and-control helicopter. With its special communications package, it can help a landing force commander maintain a broad sense of what is going on in real time. It can also play an important role in maritime special operations, combat assault, and medical evacuation. The UH-1N is scheduled to be upgraded in 2004 to include a four-blade rotor (instead of two), a state-of-the-art cockpit, night targeting, enhanced landing gear, and the ability to carry six weapons. These changes will also be made to the AH-1W Super Cobra, which shares 84 percent commonality with the UH-1N. The "beach ball" under the nose in this photo is a forward-looking infrared (FLIR) seeker with laser targeting capability.

Several resources are available to gather this intelligence. An AH-1W Super Cobra attack helicopter, an AV-8B Harrier jet, or even an unmanned aerial vehicle (UAV) like the RQ-2A Pioneer, which can launch from LPD-class ships, can fly over the beach area and take photos. Doing that, however, is likely to attract unwanted attention. A more stealthy option is to send in the nuclear attack submarine to check things out. The drawback to

doing that is the submarine could find itself in the middle of a minefield or run aground on a sandbar. Furthermore, because of its sheer size, a sub simply cannot get close enough to the beach to check everything out.

So to learn everything there is to know about the beach, the ESG commodore calls on the Marine Force Reconnaissance detachment from the embarked MEU/SOC—or perhaps even a Navy SEAL platoon or squad if one is available—to swim ashore and scout out the area. These elite teams use a variety of means to travel from the amphibious ships to the beach, including scuba, low-visibility combat rubber raiding rafts, and

Left: An LAV-25 from the 15th MEU/SOC loaded with gasoline debarks a landing craft in Kuwait under the watchful eye of the beachmaster. The Marine Corps uses a variety of landing craft to accomplish its amphibious assault mission, including LCACs and LCUs (Landing Craft, Utility). The LCU shown in this photo pulls itself free from the sand by its rear anchor. It releases the anchor as it approaches the beach and then winches itself back to sea after unloading its cargo.

Below: Flying over Afghanistan on a mission, the gunner focuses his attention on the ground for telltale signs of enemy weapons fire. The .50-caliber machine gun mounted in the window is the only weapon aboard the Sea Knight. *U.S. Navy*

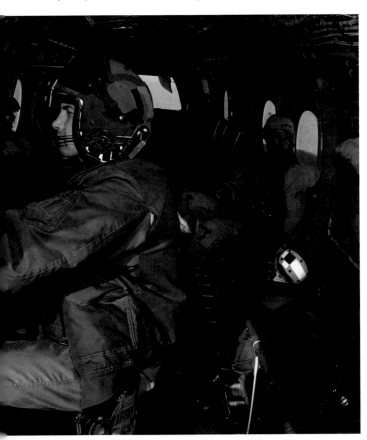

MARINE PRAYER

Almighty Father, whose command is over all and whose love never fails, make me aware of Thy presence and obedient to Thy will.

Keep me true to my best self, guarding me against dishonesty in purpose and deed, and helping me to live so that I can face my fellow Marines, my loved ones, and Thee without shame or fear.

Protect my family.

Give me the will to do the work of a Marine and to accept my share of responsibilities with vigor and enthusiasm. Grant me the courage to be proficient in my daily performance. Keep me loyal and faithful to my superiors and to the duties my country and the Marine Corps have entrusted to me.

Make me considerate of those committed to my leadership. Help me to wear my uniform with dignity, and let it remind me daily of the traditions which I must uphold.

If I am inclined to doubt, steady my faith; if I am tempted, make me strong to resist; if I should miss the mark, give me courage to try again. Guide me with the light of truth and grant me wisdom by which I may understand the answer to my prayer.

– Amen

A CH-53E Super Stallion swoops in—cargo hook extended—to conduct an external-lift operation during Operation Iraqi Freedom. The guide-man in front plays a critical role, since the pilot cannot see the other Marine, who is hidden by the yellow dust cloud kicked up by the rotors' downblast. If the outside guide were not there, the pilot would lose his situational awareness—making a crash more likely.

"Heigh ho, heigh ho, it's off to work we go." Marines assigned to the 2nd MEB walk through the well deck of the USS *Kearsarge* (LHD-3) to crawl inside a personnel and troop module that seats up to 150 Marines and their combat gear. Once they are inside, the vehicles and LAVs lined up in the well deck will drive aboard the LCAC to be secured down for the fast trip ashore. *U.S. Navy*

electric-powered, miniature submarines known as swimmer-delivery vehicles (SDV). The Mark VIII and *Gator*-class SDVs are widely used today and can be deployed worldwide aboard surface ships and submarines.

Once the collected intelligence is analyzed and an amphibious-assault plan has been drawn up, the next step is to get the Marines and their combat gear quickly and safely ashore. The best way to achieve this is through the combined use of helicopters and landing craft. The undisputed king of amphibious transport is the air-cushioned LCAC. As mentioned earlier in this chapter, the amphibs usually carry one to four of these fast and powerful craft in their well decks.

The LCAC (also known as the "Flying Frisbee" and "Flying Carpet") was designed to carry a 70-ton pay-load into a 25-knot headwind with 4- to 6-foot seas at 50 knots. It's an incredible feat of naval engineering. And since the LCAC floats about 5 feet above the ocean and land, it can gain access to 75 percent of the beaches

in the world—regardless of the coastlines' ruggedness. By comparison, conventional landing craft can land at only 15 percent of the coasts.

Almost nothing can stop this beast. Even if the containment skirt ("bag") suffers a significant tear, the LCAC can still maneuver.

Although M1A1 Abrams tanks, LAV-25 light armored vehicles, and Humvees are driven aboard the LCAC and chained down, the Marines themselves climb inside a large, windowless, metal-box container known as the personnel and troop module (PTM). The PTM seats up to 150 Marines and their combat gear. Once inside, the hatch is shut and the Marines sit like sardines waiting for the LCAC to make its quick trip from the gator to the beachhead. The purpose of the PTM is to protect the Marines from the heavy sea spray kicked-up by the LCAC slicing through the waves and to prevent anyone from being tossed over-board or, worse yet, into the enormous propeller blades positioned at the stern of the LCAC that thrust it forward.

A dramatic demonstration over Iraq of a KC-130 Hercules launching a series of hot flares that are used to detract and decoy incoming heat-seeking missiles.

An aviation boatswain's mate gives the go-ahead for an AV-8B Harrier jump jet to do a vertical takeoff from the deck of the USS *Essex* (LHD-2). This is a critical point in the procedure, because the pilot must not only safely take off, but he must do so by matching the forward speed of the *Essex*, which is still slicing through the ocean. If the pilot does not achieve this, the Harrier jet directly behind him will end up in his cockpit. If you look closely, you can see that the Harrier is already levitating a foot or so above the flight deck. The Harrier is used by the Marines for light attack and close-air support missions. *U.S. Navy*

Left: Drawing the proverbial line in the sand, a company commander uses a terrain model to brief his Marines before a raid of a secret Ba'ath Party hideout in Shamiya, Iraq, where members are suspected of planning attacks against U.S.-led coalition forces. In the subsequent raid, a half-dozen Iraqis were detained, and the Marines recovered a small cache of weapons and Ba'ath Party documents. *U.S. Army*

Right: A remotely controlled model aircraft flies over a Marine Stinger battery during a live-fire training exercise in South Korea. The Humvee in the photo is carrying the Avenger Weapon System, which consists of four Stinger missiles on each rotating arm. A turret/cockpit is located between the two arms, where a Marine aims and fires the weapon at the target. The Avenger, which is essentially a low-altitude air defense weapon, can hit targets up to altitudes of 10,000 feet, nearly 5 miles away. When necessary, the system can be operated through remote control.

Left: Weapons are loaded onto an AH-1W Super Cobra attack helicopter, which landed for a refueling near Tikrit, Iraq. Beginning in 2004, the Super Cobra is scheduled to receive a number of modifications to make it more lethal, including a composite four-blade rotor, advanced cockpit displays, digital fire control, self-contained navigation, and on-board mission planning software. The new designation for the helicopter will be AH-1Z.

Amphibious assaults are conducted in a series of "waves." This is because an expeditionary strike group does not have enough landing craft to simultaneously land 2,200 Marines. The first wave usually consists of five or six LCACs loaded with Marines who establish the point of the invasion force. These LCACs unload from their host gators and then meet up in the ocean at a "holding point" located 5 to 15 miles offshore so they cannot be seen or heard by the enemy.

When the order is given, the "Flying Carpets" align abreast one another—staggered to avoid being easy targets—and speed to the coast at 40–50 knots. Simultaneously, an air combat element (ACE) is launched from a *Tarawa*- or *Wasp*-class amphibious assault ship (a.k.a. "princess gator") to provide air cover and/or to travel inland to a landing zone and drop off a forward combat team that is tasked with conducting a specific mission. The ACE is usually composed of AH-1W Super Cobra attack helicopters, CH-46 and CH-53 troop-carrying helicopters, and AV-8B Harrier attack jets.

As the LCACs approach the beach, they are greeted by flashlight-waving members of the beach landing party, who were inserted by aircraft or other means hours or, in some instances, days earlier. The beachmaster owns the beach, and no one, not even an LCAC, can come ashore without his or her permission and guidance. When an LCAC comes ashore, it slows down to about 15 knots and zips up onto the beach; none of the Marines aboard the LCAC in the PTM feels the transition from ocean to land—the ride is that smooth.

Once ashore, the "Hopper"—as the beach landing party refers to the LCAC—spins sharply 90-degrees to

This is a close-up look at an amphibious assault vehicle (AAVP7) as it approaches the well deck of the USS *Fort McHenry* (LSD-43) during amphibious operations off the coast of the Philippines. The fully tracked vehicle is the only one in the world capable of operating in rough seas and plunging surf (up to 10 feet). In the water, it has a range of 55 miles at 8 miles per hour. For protection, it is equipped with a .50-caliber machine gun and a 40mm grenade launcher, both of which are mounted in a powered turret that can rotate 360 degrees. There are several variants of the AAV in existence, including a command vehicle and a repair/recovery vehicle. *U.S. Navy*

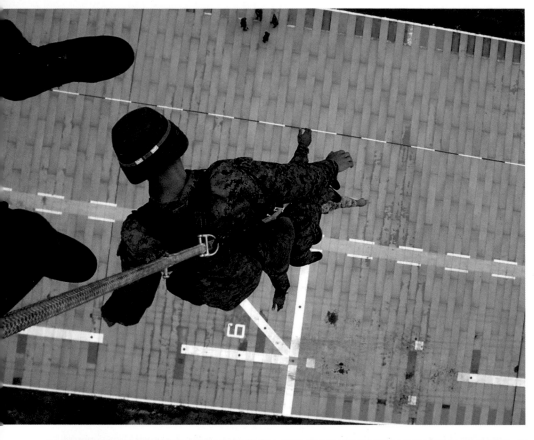

Marines learn the fine art of special purpose insertion and extraction (SPIE), a system used by special operations forces to quickly insert or extract from hostile territory. It consists of a rope suspended below a helicopter (usually a CH-46 Sea Knight); the Marines hitch themselves to it with safety harnesses. They remain suspended below the helicopter—arms outstretched for stability's sake—for the duration of the flight. SPIE can be used to transport eight or nine Marines, without their gear. Below the Marines in this photo is the layout of an amphibious assault ship. The small red dots at top are actually four instructors on the deck of the ship.

Left: An F/A-18D Hornet from Marine All-Weather Fighter Attack Squadron 242 is refueled by an Air Force KC-10 while on its way to Australia to participate in joint exercise. The Marines use the Hornet as a strike fighter, forward air controller, tactical air controller, and tactical reconnaissance aircraft. In addition, the night attack suite allows the Hornet to conduct operations in poor weather conditions at low altitudes using night-vision goggles and forward-looking infrared (FLIR) systems. Its nine external wing stations enable the aircraft to carry a plethora of weapons, including Harpoon antiship cruise missiles, Sidewinder air intercept missiles, Maverick air-to-ground missiles, and bombs—both conventional and laser-guided.

Although Force Recon Marines can swim underwater using diving equipment, occasionally the distance from ship to shore is either too far (due to the conditions at hand) or the currents are too strong. In those situations, they work with the Navy SEALs, who "drive" them ashore in a minisubmarine like the one in this photo. Once near shore, the Marines can debark and continue to do the necessary stealthy surveillance, minefield detection, and hydrographic surveys for a pending amphibious assault. *U.S. Navy*

the right in a maneuver known as a "side to." This positions the bow of the LCAC so that it is parallel to the ocean. It allows the vehicles aboard to be driven off onto hard-packed sand instead of loose sand that might cause them to get stuck. As soon as the LCAC is unloaded, it reinflates its skirt, turns about, and heads back to the amphib for the next load.

In any given amphibious assault, several landings are made. The first two waves bring ashore Marines and their amphibious assault vehicles, such as AAVP7s. It is followed by two more waves that transport Humvees armed with .50-caliber machine guns, light armored vehicles (LAV-25s), and M1A1 Abrams main battle tanks. The remaining waves—the actual number varies by the mission—bring ashore artillery (155mm howitzers) and logistical support units. The second and later waves are usually done by a host of landing craft, not just the LCAC. The more common craft include LCMs (landing craft, mechanized), LCUs (landing craft, utility) and, occasionally, LSTs (tank landing ships).

From start to finish, an expeditionary strike group can unload an entire MEU/SOC and its combat gear within 36 hours. If speed is of the essence, CH-46 and

CH-53 helicopters can be used to transport vehicles and cargo ashore, supplementing the unloading process.

If, at any time, the amphibious assault force or the forward-deployed combat team comes under enemy threat or hostile fire, the guided-missile destroyer and cruiser jump into the fray. They fire their guns and missiles at enemy positions, which are identified and called in by the Marines, the beach-landing party, or aircraft flying in the area. This is known as naval gunfire support, and its sole purpose is to protect American lives while forcing the enemy to retreat.

By the time a MEU/SOC has completely unloaded from the gators, the point components of the assault force are already several miles inland. What was initially a naval conflict has quickly metamorphosed into a land battle. From here on out, the ESG plays a supporting role to the Leathernecks in the field, providing the Marines with fire support, airlift capability, replenishment of supplies, and, if necessary, medical services aboard the amphibious assault ship. If history is any indicator, it won't be long before the expeditionary strike group is transporting the Marines back aboard, the battle or crisis having been quickly and decisively resolved.

FIVE

The United States has many elite units, such as the Army's Delta Force and the Navy's SEAL Teams, but there is only one elite fighting *force*, and that is the United States Marines. Although it is the smallest of the U.S. military branches, the Marine Corps has the greatest proportion of personnel in operational forces of any of the branches. This Marine, who is carrying an M249 squad automatic weapon, is about to participate in a live-fire training exercise on the deck of his ship. *U.S. Navy*

Anytime, Anywhere

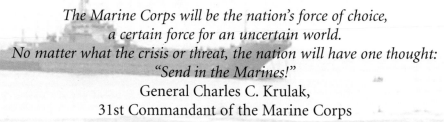

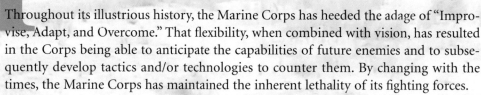

*The Marine Corps will be the nation's force of choice,
a certain force for an uncertain world.
No matter what the crisis or threat, the nation will have one thought:
"Send in the Marines!"*
General Charles C. Krulak,
31st Commandant of the Marine Corps

Throughout its illustrious history, the Marine Corps has heeded the adage of "Improvise, Adapt, and Overcome." That flexibility, when combined with vision, has resulted in the Corps being able to anticipate the capabilities of future enemies and to subsequently develop tactics and/or technologies to counter them. By changing with the times, the Marine Corps has maintained the inherent lethality of its fighting forces.

In its early years, the mission of the Corps was to serve as shipboard prize crews, sharpshooters, and landing parties. In the late 1800s and early 1900s, it found itself in several long, drawn-out peacemaking campaigns in the Caribbean region. In the 1930s and 1940s, it was heavily involved in amphibious operations. And since the end of World War II, the Marine Corps has served as a rapid-deployment force, quelling conflicts by employing close-air support and vertical envelopment techniques.

Today, the mission of the Marine Corps is once again evolving. As the tip of the spear, it is still a rapid-deployment force that is usually the "first to fight," but the emergence of ambiguous but highly dangerous terrorism, insurgency, and regional ethnic and social animosities are dramatically influencing that role. Fast military response is needed, but the enemy is no longer easily found or clearly identified. In fact, there is vague distinction among terrorist organizations, minority subgroups, insurgent factions, rogue elements, and international criminal cartels.

Furthermore, most conflicts now take place in crowded urban settings, where innocent civilians are deliberately placed in jeopardy by the combatants to hinder direct attack. Hence, *precise* lethal and nonlethal means of military response—now jointly conducted with numerous forces—are needed more than ever.

Adding to the haze is the reality that the Marine Corps plays a greater "first to respond" role today. Marines are routinely engaged in civilian evacuations, humanitarian aid missions, peacekeeping operations, enforcement duties, and homeland security issues. These assignments are by and large diametrically opposed to the expansive carnage the Marines were trained in boot camp to inflict on the battlefield. As such, noncombat operations severely test the emotional and mental fortitude of deployed Marines.

The twenty-first century Marine Corps has quickly acknowledged the changing face of warfare and has already acted to ensure that it maintains flexible and wide-ranging capabilities to deter conflict, respond to crises, and fight any enemy in the new global "insecurity" environment. In its *Marine Corps Strategy 21,* the Corps lists as its first goal the making of Marines who possess the judgment, strength of character, and ability to make sound, timely, and independent decisions in a chaotic environment that is likely to constantly change.

The second goal is to optimize the Marine Corps' ability to operate in urban and austere environments across the spectrum of conflicts (such as guerilla warfare, insurgency, and attacks involving weapons of mass destruction), while simultaneously reducing its dependence on existing infrastructure. As part of this endeavor, the Corps intends to improve its integration with allied and coalition forces, as well as to enhance its surveillance, target acquisition, fire support, and command-and-control systems, so that it can better shape the battlefield and attack the enemy's vulnerabilities. The end result is a naval expeditionary combat force that is instantly ready to assist

Left: The ramp-mounted weapon system (RMWS) is a new "toy" the Marine Corps is testing as an addition to its CH-53 Super Stallion helicopters, so they have 180 degrees of defensive fire from the rear. In the global war on terrorism in Afghanistan (Operation Enduring Freedom), the Stallions came under heavy fire by insurgents, forcing the Marines to cargo-strap themselves on the ramp so they could provide suppressive fire with their M16 service rifles. The RMWS is a .50-caliber machine gun with a 300-round magazine. It can fire 1,100 rounds per minute, twice the rate of other machine guns.

Right: As evidenced by the mud splatter, these Marines have done a bit of off-roading with this interim fast attack vehicle (IFAV), which seems reminiscent of the so-called "technicals" (civilian vehicles mounted with automatic weapons) used by rebel forces in Somalia. The agile vehicle is used by Force Recon and SCAMP Marines after landing by CH-53 Sea Stallion (or in the future, MV-22 Osprey) to conduct quick reconnaissance missions and to emplace sensors to detect enemy movement. The IFAV, which can also be delivered by parachute, is being used by Marines in Afghanistan. Notice the small "Globe and Anchor" emblem on the driver's door. Even in a combat zone, you can find the ever-popular USMC sticker, just like here in the United States on car bumpers.

allies, defeat any enemy, and convince belligerent nations of the wisdom of keeping the peace.

The last goal is to capitalize on innovative technologies, so the Marine forces can succeed in the twenty-first century. This includes evolving maneuver-warfare tactics; enhancing high-speed troop lift; improving logistical support, so it can provide rapid and precise distribution of equipment; and networking communications, information, and intelligence systems into a seamless, global structure. Among the many programs the Marine Corps is either supporting or acquiring to support joint-military force operations, are:

The sign is no joke. Marines take their guard duties very seriously, and they should, because they are often entrusted with protecting some of America's most vital military assets, such as nuclear weapons, ballistic missile submarines, command and control centers, and top-secret documents. Marines also guard U.S. embassies and consulates overseas.

NICKNAMES FOR THE MARINES

Devil Dogs (Teufelhunden)—Given to the Marines by the Germans after the battle of Belleau Wood in World War I. It refers to the ferocity with which the Marines fought; the Germans reported to headquarters they had encountered "shock troops."

Grunt—In reference to the infantryman, who uses a pack to carry everything into battle. It's not unusual for a modern combat load to weigh 125 pounds, causing its bearer to "grunt" under the weight.

Gyrene—An old term that was used in reference to the Royal Marines in the late nineteenth century, and to the U.S. Marines beginning around 1910.

Leathernecks—In reference to a very stiff and uncomfortable black leather neckpiece that was part of the U.S. Marine Corps' uniform from 1775 to 1875. The purpose of the 3-inch tall collar was to keep a Marine's head erect, although some speculate that it also served to protect a man's throat from being slashed in battle.

Seagoing Bell Hops—A rude term used by Navy sailors at the beginning of the twentieth century. Sailors also referred to Marines as "Tin Soldiers."

Soldiers of the Seas—A traditional term used to describe marines of all countries dating back to the 1600s.

The President's Own—Although this term applies officially to the Marine Band, it is also often used to refer the entire Marine Corps.

Yellow Legs—In reference to the khaki leggings worn by Marines during the Korean War. In fact, Communist forces were ordered not to attack the "Yellowlegs," but rather Army soldiers instead. The Marines, ever eager to fight, responded by removing their leggings so the enemy would not immediately flee.

Although they remind some of the winged monkeys in the movie *The Wizard of Oz*, these MV-22 Ospreys represent the future of amphibious warfare. The Marine Corps will use the Osprey to transport Marines ashore from over the horizon during an assault. It can be up-and-out of a landing zone in less than half the time it takes a CH-46 Sea Knight to depart, because it can accelerate from 0 to 280 miles per hour in just 63 seconds. The Osprey will allow the Marines to move inland more quickly and farther than is now possible with helicopters, forcing the enemy to spread its military assets over a larger area. *U.S. Navy*

• LDP-17 Amphibious Ship—As mentioned in the previous chapter, the Navy's state-of-the-art *San Antonio*-class transport ship will significantly enhance amphibious warfare. Marines will be able to more quickly project force from the sea against the enemy.

• MV-22 Osprey—This radical, $40-million vertical takeoff and landing aircraft will be able to ferry Marines long-range (200 nautical miles) from amphibious ships positioned well over the horizon against enemy forces, deep inland. Intended to replace the Marine Corps' aging CH-46E Sea Knight and CH-53D Sea Stallion medium-lift helicopters, the 360 Ospreys being purchased by the Corps will also be used for cargo lift, raid operations, logistical support, and tactical recovery of aircraft and personnel. Each is capable of carrying 24 combat-equipped Marines or a 10,000-pound external load. The MV-22's 38-foot prop-rotor system and engine/transmission nacelles,

mounted on the wing tips, allow it to function as a helicopter for takeoff and landing. When airborne, the nacelles rotate 90 degrees, thereby converting the Osprey into a turbo-prop aircraft. The eventual fielding of the MV-22 Osprey will bring Marine Corps and Air Force special operations forces closer together. Two units (VMX-22 and VMMT-204, both at MCAS New River, North Carolina) have been already established to test and evaluate the Osprey, as well as to train pilots and aircraft maintainers. In the world of covert missions, the Osprey will play a pivotal role in inserting and extracting special operations forces, including Force Recon Marines. The MV-22's ability to fly fast at low altitudes over long distances can not be matched by any other aircraft, thus making it uniquely suited for the covert world of special operations. In 2004, the Marine Corps selected 14 pilots to join the ranks of its first two MV-22 Osprey squadrons.

Left: Even when in paradise, Marines never rest. This Marine stands guard on the shoreline in Dili, East Timor, while the USS *Blue Ridge* (LCC-19) rests at anchor off shore. The *Blue Ridge* is the flagship of the commander, U.S. Seventh Fleet, and it serves as a sea-based command and control asset, directing military operations for an entire region. Not surprisingly, the ship bristles with antennas and sensors that collect and transmit intelligence data. *U.S. Navy*

Below: A platoon of Marines prepares to advance carefully over sand dunes and through the scrubby vegetation as part of a training exercise on the Binturan Range in Brunei. The experience enables the Marines to enhance their interoperability with the Royal Brunei Landing Force, as well as to hone their combat skills in near-tropical conditions.

The new expeditionary fighting vehicle (EFV) undergoes final testing before it begins to replace the Marine Corps' aging amphibious assault vehicle (AAVP7) in the 2006–2008 time frame. The EFV has twice the armor protection and three times the water speed of an AAVP7. It will serve as an important cornerstone of the twenty-first century Marine Corps' amphibious force, along with the MV-22 Osprey and the *San Antonio*-class gators.

• Expeditionary Fighting Vehicle (EFV)—This is a high-speed, armored amphibious-assault vehicle that transports infantry Marines more than 25 miles from ship to shore, and then inland to the fight. The EFV is more than three times faster than the present amphibious assault vehicle (AAV7A1) used by the Corps and has nearly twice its protective armor. It moves at 23–29 miles per hour at sea using two water jets, and 45 miles per hour on land using its tracks. Additionally, it provides nuclear, biological, and chemical protection for the 18 Marines and crew of 3, and it offers the land mobility equal to that of the agile

M1A1 Abrams tank. Its high-tech command and control system gives the Marines access to real-time intelligence and data from satellites, ships, aircraft, and other sources. Combined, these capabilities will revolutionize every facet of combat operations. The vehicle, which has a cruising range of 300 miles, can easily navigate over 8-foot trenches and 3-foot-high walls. It is armed with the Bushmaster II 30mm cannon and an M240 7.62mm machine gun. The Marine Corps intends to acquire 1,013 EFVs to replace its aging AAV7A1, with the first fighting vehicles reaching the Fleet Marine Force in 2006.

FAMOUS SAYINGS

Why the hell can't the Army do it if the Marines can? They are all the same kind of men. Why can't the Army be like the Marines?

—General John J. Pershing, U.S. Army

I can never again see a United States Marine without experiencing a feeling of reverence.

—General Johnson, U.S. Army

The more Marines I have around, the better I like it.

—General Clark, U.S. Army

Sleep easy tonight, the Marines are on duty.

—Unknown

We're surrounded. That simplifies the problem.

—Lieutenant General Lewis B. "Chesty" Puller, U.S. Marine Corps

Marine Corps integrity is doing that thing which is right, when no one is looking.

—Colonel Colin Lampard, U.S. Marine Corps

G%$#@! it, you'll never get the Purple Heart hiding in a foxhole! Follow me!

—Captain Henry P. "Jim" Crowe, U.S. Marine Corps, Guadalcanal, January 13, 1943

This was no retreat. All that happened was that we found more Chinese behind us than in front of us, so we about-faced and attacked.

—Lieutenant General "Chesty" Puller, Battle of Chosin Reservoir, Korean Conflict

They're on our right. They're on our left. They're in front of us. They're behind us. They can't get away from us this time!

—Lieutenant General "Chesty" Puller, Battle of Chosin Reservoir

Every Marine is first and foremost, a rifleman. All other conditions are secondary.

—General Alfred M. Gray, 29th Commandant of the Marine Corps

Being ready is not what matters. What matters is winning after you get there.

—General Charles C. Krulak, 31st commandant of the Marine Corps

Retreat, hell! We just got here.

—Attributed to Captain Lloyd Williams, U.S. Marine Corps, Battle of Belleau Wood in World War I, June 1918

Some people spend an entire lifetime wondering if they made a difference. The Marines don't have that problem.

—President Ronald Reagan (1985)

The Marines I have seen around the world have the cleanest bodies, the filthiest minds, the highest morale, and the lowest morals of any group of animals I have ever seen. Thank GOD for the United States Marine Corps!

—Eleanor Roosevelt (1945)

Old breed? New breed? There's not a damn bit of difference so long as it's the Marine breed.

—Lieutenant General "Chesty" Puller

Today, the world looks to America for leadership. And America looks to its Corps of Marines.

—President Ronald Reagan

There are only two kinds of people that understand Marines: Marines and the enemy. Everyone else has a second-hand opinion.

—Unknown

Once a Marine, always a Marine!

—Attributed to Master Sergeant Paul Woyshner, a 40-year Marine, who said this during a bar room argument with a discharged Marine.

They [women Marines] don't have a nickname, and they don't need one. They get their basic training in a Marine atmosphere, at a Marine Post. They inherit the traditions of the Marines. They ARE Marines.

—Lieutenant General Thomas Holcomb, U.S. Marine Corps (1943)

• High Speed Vessel (HSV)—The HSV is a high-speed (40-plus knots), shallow-draft (12 feet) catamaran naval ship that enhances the Marine Corps' ability to conduct sea-based operations in the littoral regions of the world. The 370-foot-long, multi–mission HSV can be used for mine warfare, special operations, ship-to-shore maneuvers, and humanitarian aid duties. With its impressive speed, it can move troops and equipment into a theater of operations faster than present methods allow. The Marines can use the vessel's flight deck for aviation missions (such as visit, board, search, and seizure, or VBSS) involving the MV-22 Osprey, AH-1W Super Cobra attack helicopters, and/or CH-46 or CH-53 medium lift helicopters. They can also launch and recover amphibious assault vehicles and small boats from the HSV. Two HSVs were leased by the Navy, and both successfully participated in Operation Iraqi Freedom in 2003. The USS *Swift* (HSV-2) is now part of Expeditionary Strike Group 1. The Department of the Navy continues to explore the use of high-speed ships to enable a faster, more responsive deployment of forces.

• Lightweight 155mm Howitzer (LW-155)—The world's first 155mm towed artillery howitzer that has an air-transportable weight of less than 9,800 pounds, the LW-155 features a digital fire control system, better ground mobility, and faster reaction times than its predecessor, the M198 155mm medium howitzer. Combined, these make the howitzer more lethal and easier to deploy in support of MAGTF combat forces. The LW-155 howitzer began entering service with the Marine Corps in 2003, and it will eventually replace the much heavier (15,758-pound) M198 155mm medium howitzer.

• Maritime Prepositioning Force (Future)—The MPF (F) is a joint Navy and Marine Corps project to revolutionize the arming and resupply of expeditionary combat forces in upcoming years, enabling the Marines to support themselves indefinitely from a sea base. The MPF (F) is envisioned to accomplish four functions that the current MPF does not: at-sea arrival and assembly of Marine units; direct support of the amphibious task force; the ability to sustain Marine combat forces from the sea for extended periods; and the ability to allow Marine units to regroup at sea and, subsequently, redeploy again. It will be necessary to design and build a new family of ships to provide these capabilities.

The Navy, Marine Corps, and Army are exploring the design and capability of the *Joint Venture* (HSV-X1), a high-speed, experimental catamaran that could transport 400 troops and their combat equipment over the littoral regions of the world into forward areas. The vessel's flight deck can accommodate the Marine Corps' MV-22 Osprey, CH-46 and CH-53 cargo/transport helicopters, the AH-1W Super Cobra, and the AV-8B Harrier. The *Joint Venture* was successfully deployed for military operations in Kuwait during Operation Enduring Freedom in 2003. *U.S. Navy*

Above: A Marine assigned with the 26th MEU/SOC practices his marksmanship skills at a firing range set up near Kandahar, Afghanistan. Since he is firing a scoped, M4A1 5.56 x 45mm carbine close-quarter battle weapon (CQBW) with a collapsible stock, it can be assumed he is a Force Recon Marine. Until 1998, Force Recon used the Heckler and Koch MP-5N submachine gun, but set it aside because the MP-5N could not deliver accurate fire past 50 yards. Its bullet was also unable to penetrate body armor. Although the MP-5N was a subpar weapon for combat, it is still used by Force Recon for VIP security details. Rifle aside, the preferred sidearm of Force Recon is the single-action, .45-caliber MEU/SOC pistol. During the work-up and deployment phases, it's not unusual for a Marine to fire 80,000 rounds.

Above: A KC-130 Hercules transport equipped for aerial-refueling missions of helicopters and tactical aircraft sits impatiently with its props turning as Marines from the 26th MEU/SOC race to board it. In its tanker role, the Hercules has a 1,150-mile radius with 45,000 pounds of fuel, while in its transport role it has a 3,300-mile radius with 38,258 pounds of cargo or 92 combat-equipped Marines. The plane's wing-mounted hose-and-drogue refueling pods each transfer 300 gallons per minute to two aircraft at the same time.

HOLLYWOOD MARINES

The public loves Marine movies. Who today does not recall the gruff Colonel Nathan R. Jessup, USMC, (Jack Nicholson in *A Few Good Men*) snarling in court: "You can't handle the truth! Son, we live in a world that has walls. And those walls have to be guarded by men with guns. . .

"You don't want the truth because deep down in places you don't talk about at parties, you *want* me on that wall. You *need* me on that wall. We use words like honor, code, loyalty. We use these words as the backbone of a life spent defending something. . .

"I have neither the time nor the inclination to explain myself to a man who rises and sleeps under the blanket of the very freedom that I provide and then questions the manner in which I provide it."

The first-ever Marine movie, *Star Spangled Banner*, was produced in 1916 by the Thomas Alva Edison Studio, and it featured Paul Kelly as a swashbuckling Marine. In the decades since then, Hollywood has filmed nearly 100 movies and injected Leathernecks into successful television series to quench the public's thirst for the Marine Corps. Here is a partial list of some of the better-known classics.

Movies:

55 Days at Peking
All the Young Men
Battle Cry
Death Before Dishonor
The Black Sheep
The D.I.
A Few Good Men
Fighter Attack
The Fighting Marines
Flying Leathernecks
Full Metal Jacket
Guadalcanal Diary
Gung-Ho
Halls of Montezuma
Heartbreak Ridge
Hell in the Pacific
Inchon
Marine Raiders
The Marinettes
Pride of the Marines
The Proud and the Profane

The Rock
Sands of Iwo Jima
Sniper
South Seas Paradise
Stars and Stripes Forever
Tell it to the Marines
Til The End of Time
To the Shores of Tripoli
Until They Sail
Wake Island
What Price Glory?
The Wind and The Lion

Television:

Black Sheep Squadron
   (previously *Baa-Baa Black Sheep*)
Gomer Pyle, USMC
JAG
Major Dad
Supercarrier
The Lieutenant

• High-Mobility Artillery Rocket System (HIMARS)—A rocket-launching system carried aboard an Oshkosh truck that will enable Marines to accurately engage enemy targets at longer distances than today (36 miles versus 18 miles), with a high-volume of fire in all weather conditions. HIMARS, which can be airlifted aboard C-130 Hercules transport aircraft, is capable of firing all rockets and missiles currently being used, as well as those under development. The system is composed of one launcher, two resupply vehicles, two trailers, and a basic load of nine pods (six rockets per pod). The current plan is to field two battalions in the 14th Marines, each with 18 launchers. Production of HIMARS is to begin in 2006, with full-operational capability expected in 2008.

• F-35 Joint Strike Fighter—This is the next-generation strike-fighter being built by Lockheed Martin for the Marine Corps, Air Force, and Navy—and it will replace the Marines' aging AV-8B Harrier attack jet and F/A-18A/C/D Hornet fighter jets. The stealthy F-35 will be produced with three slightly different variants: a conventional variant for the Air Force, an aircraft carrier variant for the Navy, and a short takeoff and vertical-landing variant (STOVL) for the Marine Corps. The latter, which can hover in midair, is designed to meet the Marines' requirement that it be able to operate from large-deck amphibious ships, forward-operating bases, and austere environments. By doing so, the Marines will be able to access three to five times more airfields around the world than with existing aircraft. The STOVL is able to take off from land or sea, fly at supersonic cruise, accomplish its mission with advanced electronics and weapons, and then return to its expeditionary site. The Navy and Marine Corps will buy 680 aircraft; a decision has yet to be made as to how those will be divided between the two services. Initial low-rate production of the first STOVLs will begin in 2006.

The Joint Strike Fighter program, which began in the early 1990s, is intended to create a highly survivable strike fighter that can meet the combat needs of the Navy, Marine Corps, and Air Force in the twenty-first century. In 2001, the U.S. Department of Defense selected Lockheed Martin's F-35 aircraft design as the winner; the short-takeoff and vertical landing (STOVL) version is shown in this photo. It is a stealthy, supersonic, multirole fighter capable of carrying two air-to-air and two precision air-to-surface missiles in an internal bay plus 15,000 pounds of armaments and two missiles externally. The Marine's STOVL version is unique because to come to a hover, a door behind the pilot opens to reveal a vertical thruster, which produces 39,700 pounds of downward thrust. Complementing this effort, the F-35's exhaust nozzle rotates downward so that, working together, the fighter can come to a slow and controlled vertical landing.
Lockheed Martin Aeronautics Company

Given present disturbing world conditions, the Marine Corps found itself wondering, "How do you handle large crowds of armed and angry people without having any Marines injured or, worse yet, killed?" The answer is the Gladiator, an unmanned ground vehicle with day and night cameras that serves as a "Robo-cop" with attitude. It dispenses smoke and tear gas, and it is armed with either a 5.56mm light machine gun, 7.62mm machine gun, or 9mm Uzi. It essentially can perform the duties of an entire rifle company, nearly 160 Marines. The Marine Corps intends to distribute 192 Gladiators beginning in 2007 to each of its seven MEUs.

WARRIOR "TOYS"

Supplementing these major acquisitions are a plethora of smaller, but equally important, research and development projects that will uphold the Marine Corps' combat advantage over its adversaries. These include such things as the P-90 submachine gun, a compact and ergonomically designed weapon that may replace the 9mm Beretta pistol Marines currently use. The P-90 remedies the Beretta's lack of range, penetration, and ammunition capacity. Its 50-round magazine offers a lot of "solutions" to address most threats, and each round can perforate 48 plies of Kevlar bullet-resistant material from a range of up to 200 meters. The ambidextrous weapon is light, quick to aim, and easy to shoot. It promises to give Leathernecks the firepower of a submachine gun when needed.

Another area of interest to the Marines is robotics. There are a number of cutting-edge robots under development that have potential use on the battlefield to collect intelligence, provide perimeter security, or render safe an explosive device. One new unmanned aerial vehicle is the Dragon Eye, a 5-pound, backpack-portable, battery-operated spy plane the Marines can send aloft within minutes to scout the terrain ahead of a unit to locate enemy positions and obstacles. Marines view the real-time video stream through a special pair of goggles. They can also deploy the Dragon Runner, an extremely rugged radio-controlled, model-truck-like vehicle that zips through the brush and over the sand dunes to collect intelligence.

In spite of these and other great "toys," the Marine Corps knows that battles are won by Marines, not weapons or technology. And a tired Marine is not at his fighting best. So arguably the most important thing being done today is reducing the weight of a Marine's pack.

Although studies prove that a Marine should carry no more than 30 percent of his weight (50 pounds on average), Marines have entered battle humping packs weighing as much as 140 pounds. The extra weight not only takes a physical toll on the body, but it also dulls

Right: A Force Recon Marine, armed with the M4 carbine and MEU/SOC .45-caliber handgun, secures the bridge of the MV *Pvt. Franklin J. Phillips* during a ship VBSS (Visit, Board, Search, and Seizure) training mission in search of contraband, weapons, and combatants. His team fast-roped from a CH-46 helicopter onto the ship while AH-1W Super Cobra attack helicopters provided air cover and acted as a noisy diversion. Once aboard, the Marines quickly secured the engine room and bridge to stop the ship's progress. The *Pvt. Phillips* is actually part of Maritime Prepositioning Squadron Three, which equips the Marine Corps when it deploys for combat overseas. The equipment stored in a single MPF squadron is the equivalent of more than 3,000 airlift sorties. The ships can off-load either pier side or at sea. *U.S. Navy*

Left: An aircraft mechanic assigned to Marine Unmanned Aerial Vehicle Squadron 1 takes a fuel sample from an RQ-2A Pioneer during Operation Iraqi Freedom. Using its onboard camera equipment, the Pioneer performs a wide variety of reconnaissance, target-acquisition, and battle-damage assessments. It broadcasts the images in real-time back to battlefield commanders. The aircraft's low radar cross-section, low infrared signature, and remote-control versatility help protect it from enemy fire. Measuring 14 feet long, with a 16.9-foot wingspan, the Pioneer has a range of over 115 miles and can fly as high as 15,000 feet. It has a maximum speed of 110 miles per hour. They are generally deployed aboard the *Austin*-class (LPD-4) amphibious transport dock ships, where they take off and conduct missions over the horizon. *U.S. Army*

Beginning in 2004, the Marine Corps replaced its unreliable MOLLE pack with a larger and more comfortable pack made by Arc'Teryx. It consists of an internal-frame main ruck that holds 4,500 cubic inches of gear, a patrol pack (1,500 cubic inches), and a water bladder that holds 100 ounces. The pack will also hold mortar rounds outside the main pack without interfering with movement. At the time of this writing, a contest was under way to name the new combat pack.

With U.S. flags waving proudly in the breeze, a lone Marine sits among amphibious assault vehicles (AAVP7s) in a parking lot at Camp Patriot, Kuwait, as they are prepared for their return to the United States after having served in Operation Iraqi Freedom. *U.S. Navy*

mental capacity. In fact, a Marine who carries a heavy pack quickly loses situational awareness—thereby endangering himself and his fellow Marines.

To address this problem, the Marine Corps trashed the MOLLE pack (its external frame broke too frequently) and, after extensive biometrics testing, replaced it with a more reliable and comfortable, yet larger, pack made by Arc'Teryx. The Corps also drafted guidelines that specify what type of gear is to be carried in different situations. The "assault load" is the lightest pack, at 47.8 pounds, and includes only those items needed to fight, such as rifle, ammo, bayonet, camouflage paint stick, and hand grenades.

An "approach march load" weighs 71.1 pounds, and enables an average infantry Marine to hike 20 miles in eight hours while maintaining 90 percent combat effectiveness. The load includes the assault items, plus extra clothing, an entrenching tool, and three meals.

A "sustained march load" is similar to the approach load, but it assumes the Marines will not be resupplied for at least three days. As a result, it weighs in at 93.9 pounds. Marines carrying this load are to dump it immediately if they come under enemy fire so they can maneuver more easily.

The heaviest pack load is the 138-pound "existence load." It is only used when Marines do not know when they will be resupplied. It was this type of load that Marines of Task Force 58 took into Afghanistan in November 2001 when they seized Camp Rhino. The existence load is essentially a mule pack—Marines carry it when embarking or debarking aircraft or amphibious assault craft, and when going from a landing zone to a secure area. It is not intended to be carried over longer distances.

Eliminating the ponderous packs should have a significant impact on morale. It will also keep infantry Marines alert and focused on battlefield events.

In a world where the use of weapons of mass destruction is a growing threat, the Marines must be ever prepared to respond or fight in an environment laced with chemical, biological, or radiological materials. The Marines in this photo are practicing decontamination procedures. In a real chemical or biological incident, the Marine Corps' highly trained and specially equipped Chemical/Biological Incident Response Force (CBIRF) would respond. It can provide medical triage and antidotes for 1,500 nerve agent casualties, and can decontaminate 450 ambulatory casualties per hour. *U.S. Navy*

TO INFINITY AND BEYOND...

Looking further down the road, the Marine Corps is seeking to replace its light armored vehicle (LAV-25) and M1A1 Abrams tank in the 2018–2022 time frame with a new family of fighting vehicles. But the most amazing development is that the Marine Corps is actually hoping to venture into space, as characterized in the 1986 film, *Aliens*.

In that movie, a team of Marines fly across the galaxy in a spacecraft to rescue planetary pioneers who are being stalked by ravenous creatures. Dropping to the planet's surface via a shuttle, the Marines—toting high-tech weapons—conduct a daunting search-and-destroy mission.

While it seemed far-fetched nearly 20-years ago, that fantasy may well become reality. By 2030, the Marine Corps hopes to develop a hypersonic space plane that can transport Marines to any crisis spot on the globe within two hours. Known as SUSTAIN (small unit space transport and insertion), the craft would make a conventional takeoff from an airport and use scramjet engines to reach an altitude of 40 miles above the earth, moving at about Mach 10 (which equates to nearly 2 miles per second). It then shuts down the engines and coasts to a lower altitude—about 20 miles—where the engines are briefly fired up, propelling the aircraft back into space. This on-and-off process—referred to as "skipping" by scientists—continues until the plane reaches

Left: A Marine from the 22nd MEU/SOC fast-ropes from a UH-1N helo into a small room during a helicopter rope suspension training (HRST) masters course. This two-week-long course, which is taught by the Marine Corps' elite Special Operations Training Group, teaches Marines how to rig helicopters for fast-roping, SPIE, and rappelling. Using those techniques, the Marines can help insert or extract Marines, sailors, and special operations forces into even the most remote and difficult situations, such as thick forests, congested urban sprawl, or narrow mountain passes.

Right: Riding in a rigid assault craft, Marines from a small craft company begin a 90-mile journey up the Río Paraguay. It is part of a joint military operation that allows the Marines to train with Bolivian and Paraguayan forces in riverine operations.

An F/A-18 Hornet releases Mk. 83 1,000-pound bombs as part of a test to see if the bombs drop cleanly without hitting the advanced targeting forward-looking infrared (ATFLIR) sensor, which is mounted on the underside of the fighter near the bombs. The ATFLIR is a superadvanced infrared-targeting system that detects, classifies, and tracks targets in the air and on the ground. It is used to precisely hit enemy targets with a laser-guided bomb (or other ordnance) at night and in poor weather conditions. The sensor entered service in F/A-18 squadrons in late 2003. *U.S. Navy*

Marines are trained in riot-control techniques as well as use of nonlethal weapons, like this 40mm grenade round that is filled with small rubber balls. It is fired from a grenade launcher affixed to a Marine's M16 rifle. The balls disperse into a large spread to knock down and bruise rioters, encouraging them to leave the protest area. A nonlethal weapons and tactics course is taught at Camp Lejeune and Camp Pendleton, and it is usually attended by ground-combat elements of a MEU/SOC.

This is a close-up look at the Dragon Runner remotely controlled vehicle the Marine Corps purchased to assist with real-time collection of surveillance information on the battlefield. Equipped with camera sensors, the backpackable dragon is sent over hills and through brush to find hazards the Marine unit should be aware of.

its destination. Then it simply drops out of the sky and lands at an airport, deploying the Marine detachment.

To illustrate the effectiveness of this concept, the Marines could fly from MCAS Cherry Point, near Camp Lejeune in North Carolina, and arrive in Baghdad, Iraq, just 73 minutes later. The 6,420 mile journey would require only 19 "skips" off the upper atmosphere.

Such "out of the box" thinking will revolutionize warfare if, of course, the aircraft can actually be built. An express combat force of Marines presents numerous possibilities. For instance, it could quell a crisis before a larger military force is needed. Or it could rescue hostages before the captors are truly in control. Or it could evacuate embassy personnel before the building is overrun.

Although some may scoff at the idea of "Space Marines," on March 27, 2004, NASA launched the experimental X-43A jet, which used scramjets to achieve a record-setting speed of Mach 7—about 5,000 miles per hour. It was the first time an air-breathing aircraft had ever traveled so fast. (The rocket-powered X-15 hit Mach 6.7 in 1967.)

Although it appears the windows of this Humvee were shot at, they were in fact damaged by rocks and bottles tossed by a mob of angry Iraqis in the town of Karbala. The Marine trains his 5.56mm light machine gun at the crowd while other members of the 870th Military Police Company bring peace and order to the situation before it flares up.

MARINE, BY GOD

The U.S. Marine Corps is over 225 years of romping, stomping, hell, death and destruction. It is the finest fighting machine the world has ever seen. We were born in a bomb crater, our mother was an M16, and our father was the devil.

Each moment that I live is an additional threat upon your life. I am a rough-looking, roving soldier of the sea. I am cocky, self-centered, and overbearing. I do not know the meaning of fear, for I am fear itself.

I am a green, amphibious monster made of blood and guts who arose from the sea, festering on anti-Americans throughout the globe. Whenever it may arise, and when my time comes, I will die a glorious death on the battlefield, giving my life to Mom, the Corps, and the American flag.

We stole the eagle from the Air Force, the anchor from the Navy, and the rope from the Army. On the Seventh Day, while God rested, we overran His perimeter and stole the globe, and we've been running the show ever since.

We live like soldiers, talk like sailors, and slap the hell out of both of them. Soldier by day, lover by night, drunkard by choice, MARINE BY GOD!

—Author Unknown

TAPS

To all Marines past, present, and future, Americans honor your dedication and sacrifice to preserve our way of life and to keep the United States of America free. This poem, written by Medal of Honor recipient Audie L. Murphy in 1948, commemorates those who have given their lives as the ultimate sacrifice to our nation.

Alone and Far Removed

Alone and far removed from earthly care
The noble ruins of men lie buried here.
You are strong men, good men
Endowed with youth and much the will to live.
I hear no protest from the mute lips of the dead.
They rest: there is no more to give.

So long my comrades,
Sleep ye where you fell upon the field.
But tread softly, please
March O'er my heart with ease.
March on and on,
But to God alone we kneel.

Above: An illustration depicting the role the new *San Antonio-*class (LPD-17) amphibious assault ship will play in future sea-based operations. The ships can accommodate more than 700 Marines, two LCACs, and 14 expeditionary fighting vehicles, plus a slew of aircraft. They are the first naval vessels whose masts, antennas, and sensors are enclosed within an eight-sided composite structure layered with a frequency-selective surface that allows only the radio frequencies of the equipment to be transmitted. And just like the F-117 and B-2 stealth aircraft, the angled and faceted structure enclosing the ship's mast limits the enemy's ability to detect the LPD-17 by radar. To commemorate the lives of those killed in the September 11, 2001, terrorist attack, LPD-21 is named the *New York*. Twenty-four tons of steel from the World Trade Center were salvaged and melted down to make the ship's bow stem—the foremost section of the hull on the water line that slices through the water. *Raytheon*

Right: The moon shines over Kandahar. The reach of the Marine Corps today is so expansive that while Marines watch the sun rise in one region of the world, others watch the moon rise in another. *U.S. Navy*

Saying good-bye is never easy. For the Marines who live aboard cramped amphibious ships for six (or more!) months at a time when deployed (also known as a "float"), it can be a lonely and monotonous experience. For the families left behind, it can be a trying period of raising children, managing finances, and keeping spirits high. But fortunately, modern technology like the Internet and cell phones enable Marines and their loved ones to maintain regular contact. To alleviate boredom aboard ship, the Marines exercise and watch movies when not doing combat-related drills on deck.

Since 1957, the Marine pilots of Helicopter Squadron One (HMX-1) have been entrusted with transporting the president of the United States and senior government officials. Only two helicopters are approved today for this purpose—the SH-3 Sea King (partly shown in this photo) and the VH-60N Whitehawk. Both are kept in superior condition, and are serviced after every 150 hours of flight time. The aircraft are kept by the Executive Flight Detachment at Marine Corps Air Facility Quantico in Virginia and Anacostia Naval Station in Washington, D.C. When the president is aboard, the helicopter's call sign is Marine One.

With the success of this flight, scientists are encouraged that a hypersonic plane can actually be built. The Department of Defense is assisting NASA with the technology, because it sees the possibility of using it on future bombers to strike enemy forces within hours. As for the Marines, the X-43A is the first step to the heavens . . . and to putting their boots on the ground anywhere on earth.

PROUD TO SERVE

For more than 200 years, the Marine Corps has dedicated itself to protecting the interests of the United States of America. And it has done so by simply focusing on two important and demanding tasks, as affirmed in the "Strategic Concept for a Corps of Marines":

The Marine Corps' most important responsibility is to win our nation's battles. We exist because the American people and the Congress expect their Marines to provide a lean, ready, and professional fighting force—a force that guarantees success when committed.

Today, we provide such a force.

Regardless of how good we are today, the Marine Corps is committed to being better tomorrow. Innovation, ingenuity, and a willingness to continually adapt to changes across the spectrum of conflict will take Marine Corps organizations and operational thinking into the twenty-first century. Whatever the future brings, however, one thing will remain constant: *We will be ready whenever the nation says, "Send in the Marines!"*

Our second most important responsibility to the American people is to make Marines. Our ability to win our nation's battles rests, as it always has, on the individual Marine. Regardless of the relentless pace of technology, people, not machines, decide the course of battles. Our basic tenet of "Every Marine a Rifleman" reflects this firm belief.

Because people are our most precious asset, how we recruit them, train them, instill in them our core values, and equip them, will forever be our institutional focus. We take America's young men and women and imbue in them our ethos, our core values, and the skills necessary to win on the chaotic battlefield of the twenty-first century—we transform them into Marines.

This transformation process lasts forever. It begins with the recruiter and continues throughout a Marine's time in our Corps, be it 4 or 34 years. And when they leave the Corps, our Marines return to America, better for having been a U.S. Marine.

And America IS better for having a Corps of Marines. As our nation's "First to fight" and "First to respond" force-in-readiness, the Marine Corps has kept us all free. And *that* is what it means to be a U.S. Marine.

Semper Fidelis!

Secretary of State Colin Powell receives a commemorative plaque and unit coin from the commanding officer of the Marine Security Guard Battalion following the graduation of Class 5-03 after six weeks of intensive training. The Marine Corps provides security at U.S. embassies and consulates worldwide. A tour typically lasts 30 months: half in a soft post (such as Europe) and the remainder in a hardship post (Pakistan, for example). Marine Security Guards in grade E-5 and lower agree not to marry during their two consecutive 15-month tours in the program.

Appendix: Marine Speak

Aye, Aye Sir—An acknowledgment that an order has been received, understood, and that it will be carried out. It is *not* the equivalent of "yes."

Bag—Nickname for the inflatable skirt found on an LCAC.

BAM—Broad-Assed Marine, slang for a female Marine.

Bat Turn—Pilot slang for an extremely sharp turn or bank.

Bent Gun—A helicopter brevity code meaning a weapon has malfunctioned or is unsafe to use until further notice. This code is followed by the gun position (i.e., "Bent gun, left side").

Blue Book—Nickname for the *Combined List of Officers on Active Duty in the Marine Corps*, a document that lists in numerical order the rank and precedence of all Marine officers. It determines the seniority of one officer over another, based on rank and on the date of appointment within a grade.

Blues—The Marine Corps' full-dress uniform.

Bogie—Any aircraft not positively identified as friendly.

Boot—Slang for a recruit.

Brass—Slang for officers.

Brightwork—The metallic features of a uniform (e.g., belt buckle, insignia), which must remain spotless and shiny.

Brownbagger—A Marine who is married.

Bulkhead—Wall

Butter Bar—See Gold Bar.

Cammies—Camouflage field uniforms (also called Pixies, due to the new computer-generated, pixel-pattern design).

Cannon Cocker—An artilleryman.

Close Trail—Two or more aircraft staggered one behind the other.

Colors—(1) The U.S. flag; (2) The ceremonies of raising and lowering the flag.

Corpsman—A Navy medic who serves with the Marines.

Cover—A Marine's hat or cap.

Cranial Amputation—Slang for the shaved "haircut" given recruits at Boot Camp.

Cruise—The period of an enlistment.

D and D—Drunk and disorderly.

Dark Green—Slang for a black Marine. Conversely, a caucasian Marine is referred to as "Light Green."

Deuce Gear—The basic equipment carried by a Marine, as outlined in Regulation 782.

Devil Doc—Nickname for a corpsman.

Doggie—What the Marines call an enlisted soldier in the Army, in reference to "dog face."

Double Trouble—See Quad Body.

Drop Point—A point within a landing zone where helicopters are not able to land because of the rough terrain, but in which they can unload cargo or Marines while in a hover.

Dual Cool—See Quad Body.

Fast Mover—Slang for a military jet.

Feet Dry—Aircraft is over land.

Feet Wet—Aircraft is over water.

Field Day—The portion of a day set aside for barracks clean-up.

Fleet Marine Force—The land assault component of a naval expeditionary force. There are two fleet Marine forces: one assigned to the U.S. Atlantic Command and the other to the U.S. Pacific Command. Each FMF has three divisions and three wings.

Flight—Formation of two or more aircraft.

Float—Nickname for the deployment period of an amphibious ready group.

Football—Nickname for the housing atop the EA-6B Prowler's tailfin that contains antenna receivers.

Frock—To grant official permission for an officer to assume the style, title, uniform, and authority of the next higher grade.

Frog—Nickname for the CH-46 Sea Stallion, since it resembles a crouching frog.

Gangway—An order meaning "Clear a path" or "Move out of the way."

Gator—Nickname for an amphibious ship and, by extension, the sailors aboard. The word comes from "alligator."

Gear Guard—At boot camp, a Marine who is responsible for watching over the weapons and equipment of other Marines participating in a training session.

Goat Locker—The quarters of senior noncommissioned officers.

God Box—The chapel.

Gold Bar—Nickname for a second lieutenant, the lowest-ranking commissioned officer. The insignia of rank is a single gold bar. Because of a "Second Louie's" inexperience, he or she is much maligned by other officers. Other nicknames include: Butter Bar, Missing Link, Second Balloon, and Second John.

Gomer—Nickname for a new recruit, especially one that is slow, dull, or seemingly stupid. The word probably stems from the old *Gomer Pyle, USMC* television series.

Grape—Nickname for a new recruit, in reference to his shaved head.

Grunt—Nickname for an infantryman.

Gung Ho (Hard Charger)—A highly motivated, persistent, and eager Marine. A hard charger is a Marine with a gung-ho mentality, but who also has a lot of push and an abrasive personality to boot.

Gungi Marine (pronounced Gun-ji)—The type of Marine every other Marine wants on a combat mission or in a fighting position with him. A Gungi Marine is the epitome of what a Marine ought to be: honest, loyal, cunning, trustworthy, and strong. He possesses a good sense of humor and knows when to be aggressive and when to exercise caution. He has a knack for knowing how to fight and defeat the enemy, even when outnumbered.

Gunny—Nickname for a Gunnery Sergeant (E-7), who is often the senior noncommissioned officer of a unit the size of a company (or larger).

Gun Run—A strafing run (machine gun or cannon fire) made by either a fixed-wing aircraft or a helicopter gunship against a specific target or area.

Guns—(1) Nickname for the pilot of a helicopter gunship. (2) A Marine Corps weapons squad.

Gunship (Gun Bird)—A helicopter armed with rockets, missiles, etc., whose primary mission role is to attack enemy targets and/or provide close-air support to friendly ground troops.

GWOT—Global War On Terrorism

Hangar Queen—Pilot slang for an aircraft that never seems to get out of the hangar, either because it is in need of repair or because it is habitually scavenged for spare parts for other aircraft.

Hashmark—A longevity stripe found on the uniform sleeves of senior enlisted personnel. Each stripe represents the completion of an honorable four-year enlistment.

Hat—Nickname for a drill instructor.

Heel-and-Toe Watch—A condition in which one watch-stander relieves the other, and vice versa.

Helo-Cast—A fast insertion technique by which Marines jump from a slow-moving helicopter into the water.

High and Tight (also called Whitewalls)—The standard Marine haircut: cut close on the sides and only a quarter-inch or so of hair on top.

Hippo—Nickname for the AAV since it resembles the wallowing animal when motoring through the ocean.

Hollywood Marine—Nickname for a Marine who goes through basic training at MCRD San Diego rather than at MCRD Parris Island. The perception among the PI Marines is that the training is less rigorous and stressful reflecting the California lifestyle.

Hot Pump—Slang for a Helicopter In-Flight Refueling (HIFR), a technique in which a helicopter hovers over a ship while being refueled.

Hump—To march (e.g., "We humped two klicks to the galley").

In Hack—Under arrest.

Junk on the Bunk—To display clothing and/or equipment on one's bunk for inspection.

Klick—A kilometer.

Lock-On—Target is being automatically tracked by radar or gunsight.

Maggie's Drawers—A pole with a red disk affixed to it that is waved in front of a rifle target to indicate a missed shot.

Missing Link—See Gold Bar.

Mount Out—To load and embark for expeditionary service with an Amphibious Ready Group.

MRE—Meal, Ready to Eat (also jokingly referred to as "Meals Rarely Eaten" and "Meals Rejected by Everyone"), a precooked meal packaged in a triple-layer foil and plastic pouch that can be stored for up to five years, depending on temperature.

Mustang—An enlisted person who becomes an officer.

Nugget—Nickname for a rookie aviator.

Officer's Country—Any portion of a ship, post, or station that is reserved for the exclusive use of officers.

Old Salt—(1) A Marine who has been with the Corps for a long time; (2) A person who thinks he/she knows it all.

Over the Hump—More than halfway through an enlistment period.

Pickle—Slang for a Marine recruit in basic training who has been issued his or her green-colored uniform, but no name tag. When the name tag is finally received, the recruit is said to be "canned."

Pickle Button—The bomb-release button found on the control stick of a fighter-bomber aircraft.

Pickle Meadow—Nickname for the Marine Corps' Mountain Warfare Training Center located at Bridgeport, California.

Piss Call—An old naval courtesy extended to sleeping, off-duty watch personnel: They are awakened to use the latrine before it is closed for inspection or for repairs. By doing this, they will not have full bladders when they arise at their normal time . . . only to be confronted with a "Closed" sign.

Police—A verb meaning to clean up.

Poolee—Nickname for a new Marine Corps enlistee who is waiting to be sent off to recruit training, usually 3 to 12 months in the future. This limbo between civilian life and entering the Marine Corps is referred to as "being in the pool."

Purple Shaft (Order of the Purple Shaft)—Slang meaning to receive unfair treatment. The common implication is that the shaft is rammed up one's anus. The phrase is a word play on the Purple Heart Medal, which is awarded to those injured or killed in combat. On occasions involving grossly unfair treatment, the Purple Shaft is awarded with "barbed wire clusters" or "horseshit clusters."

Quad Body—A Force Recon Marine who has received special training in four areas: jump, scuba, the Army's Ranger School, and the British Royal Marines' Commando School. A Marine who is qualified in jump and scuba is known as either "Dual Cool" or "Double Trouble." When Rangers training is added, he becomes a "Triple Threat."

Rack Out—To go to bed.

Red Dog—An alert used by combat swim instructors meaning a Marine in the water is in a life-threatening situation and needs immediate rescue.

RHIP—Rank Has Its Privileges.

Rock—Nickname for Okinawa.

Rockers—Nickname for the arcs found on senior NCO sleeve insignia beneath the chevrons. When a Marine sergeant is promoted to Staff Sergeant (E-6), a rocker is added beneath the three chevrons to denote the new rank. When this happens, the Marine is said to "get his first rocker." The term refers to a rocking chair, since the more rockers a sergeant has, the older and closer to retirement he is.

Rustbucket—Nickname for an old, worn-out ship.

Saddle Up—An order meaning to put on packs and prepare to move out.

Salad Bar—Slang for the colorful service ribbons worn on a uniform.

Salty—An experienced and seasoned Marine, regardless of rank.

Scrambled Eggs—The gold decoration on the visor of an officer's hat—grade 0-4 and up. Also referred to as "chicken guts."

Scuz Rag—A cloth that is used for cleaning.

Second Balloon—See Gold Bar.

Second Hat—Nickname for the assistant drill instructor in charge of instruction.

Second John—See Gold Bar.

Secure—To put something away, or to stop doing an activity.

Semper Fu—Slang (and word play on "Semper Fi") for the Marine's new hand-to-hand combat program, which incorporates martial arts.

Sergeant Rock—Slang for a strong, aggressive, and cunning Marine who is not afraid to tackle a difficult combat mission. Named after the popular DC Comic book commando by the same name. See also Gungi Marine.

Ship Over—To re-enlist.

Side To—A maneuver an LCAC makes when landing on the beach. The craft turns abruptly to the left or right so that it is parallel to the ocean. This enables vehicles to drive off the LCAC onto the hard-packed beach.

Six, Six, and a Kick—A phrase meaning to be placed in the brig (jail) for six months, lose six months of pay, and then to be kicked out of the Marine Corps with a Bad Conduct Discharge.

Skipper—The commanding officer.

Snow—(1) To intentionally fool or mislead someone; (2) To exaggerate.

Squared Away—Everything is neat and in order.

Steel Beach Picnic—When a ship either anchors or comes to a halt and the crew—including Marines—is allowed to swim off the stern. Such a festive event is often accompanied by lunch or dinner served topside.

Third Hat—Nickname for the assistant drill instructor in charge of discipline.

Tonka—Nickname for the crane found aboard amphibious assault ships, used to remove burning aircraft or unstable ordnance from the flight deck and dump it into the ocean.

Top—Nickname for the First Sergeant.

Triple Threat—See Quad Body.

Twenty-nine Stumps—Slang for Twenty-nine Palms Marine Corps Air-Ground Combat Center, located in California's Mojave Desert.

UNREP—Underway replenishment, the resupplying and refueling of ships at sea. The replenishment ship pulls alongside the target ship and, using strung cables, sends across provisions and fuel lines.

Utes—Pronounced, "you-tees," this is short for utilities—the pixilated camouflaged clothing most often worn by Marines.

VERTREP—Vertical replenishment, the resupplying of ships at sea using helicopters. The provisions are slung beneath the helicopter in a special cargo net.

Wardroom—(1) The officers' dining area and lounge aboard a ship; (2) Officers in general.

Wet Down—To serve drinks in honor of someone's promotion. A party celebrating the same event is referred to as a "Wetting Down."

Whitewalls—See High and Tight.

Wing Wiper—An enlisted aviation Marine.

WOPS—Water operations.

Index

To Be a U.S. Air Force Pilot
ISBN 0-7603-1791-7

To Be a U.S. Army Ranger
ISBN 0-7603-1314-8

To Be a U.S. Navy SEAL
ISBN 0-7603-1404-7

Desert Dogs
ISBN 0-7603-2012-8

Marine Force Recon
ISBN 0-7603-1011-4

Praying for Slack
ISBN 0-7603-2050-0

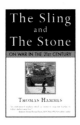

The Sling and the Stone
ISBN 0-7603-2059-4

The Threadbare Buzzard
ISBN 0-7603-2055-1

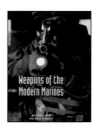

Weapons of the Modern Marines
ISBN 0-7603-1697-x